The Rhetoric of Criticism

From Hobbes to Coleridge

Other Titles of Interest

BAUM, F. A.
Montesquieu and Social Theory

BUNGE, M.
The Mind-Body Problem

HARRIS, R.
Approaches to Language

RICHARDS, T. J.
The Language of Reason

ROY, R.
Experimenting with Truth

STOVE, D.
Popper and After - Four Modern Irrationalists

TALMOR, E.
Descartes and Hume

TALMOR, E.
Mind and Political Concepts

TALMOR, E.
Language and Ethics

TALMOR, S.
Glanvill: The Uses and Abuses of Scepticism

A Pergamon Journal of Related Interest

HISTORY OF EUROPEAN IDEAS *
Editor: Dr Ezra Talmor, Haifa University, Israel

History of European Ideas is a multidisciplinary journal devoted to the study of the history of the cultural exchange between European nations and the influence of this exchange on the formation of European ideas and the emergence of the idea of Europe. The journal publishes regular review articles as well as a book review section; it also contains current information about European scholarly meetings and publications.

* Free specimen copies available upon request

The Rhetoric of Criticism

From Hobbes to Coleridge

by

SASCHA TALMOR

PERGAMON PRESS

OXFORD · NEW YORK · TORONTO · SYDNEY · PARIS · FRANKFURT

U.K.	Pergamon Press Ltd., Headington Hill Hall, Oxford OX3 OBW, England
U.S.A.	Pergamon Press Inc., Maxwell House, Fairview Park, Elmsford, New York 10523, U.S.A.
CANADA	Pergamon Press Canada Ltd., Suite 104, 150 Consumers Road, Willowdale, Ontario M2J 1P9, Canada
AUSTRALIA	Pergamon Press (Aust.) Pty. Ltd., P.O. Box 544, Potts Point, N.S.W. 2011, Australia
FRANCE	Pergamon Press SARL, 24 rue des Ecoles, 75240 Paris, Cedex 05, France
FEDERAL REPUBLIC OF GERMANY	Pergamon Press GmbH, Hammerweg 6, D-6242 Kronberg-Taunus, Federal Republic of Germany

First edition 1984

Library of Congress Cataloging in Publication Data
Talmor, Sascha.
The rhetoric of criticism.
Bibliography
Includes index.
1. Criticism–Great Britain–History.
2. Rhetoric–1500-1800. I. Title.
PR63.T34   1983   801'.95'0941   83-13390

British Library Cataloguing in Publication Data
Talmor, Sascha
The rhetoric of criticism.
1. English literature – Early modern (to 1700)
– History and criticism   2. English literature
– 18th Century – History and criticism
3. English literature – 19th century – History and criticism
I. Title
820.9   PR421
ISBN 0-08-030846-5

In order to make this volume available as economically and as rapidly as possible the author's typescript has been reproduced in its original form. This method unfortunately has its typographical limitations but it is hoped that they in no way distract the reader.

Printed in Great Britain by A. Wheaton & Co. Ltd., Exeter

To my Mother

"Our world — remembered, imagined, or perceived is organized by the language we speak."

"Our world takes shape in the evolution of our language."

(W. Haas, *The Theory of Translation*)

Preface

This book is a critical examination of the changes that occurred in English literary criticism in the seventeenth and eighteenth centuries.

Most modern commentators emphasise the psychological approach to aesthetic and critical problems which started with Hobbes and came to its culmination in Coleridge and Wordsworth. Tracing the Romantic interest in psychological phenomena and artistic creation to Hobbes's theory of the imagination and the association of ideas, they examine Neoclassical criticism in the light of a specific psychological method and terminology.

In contrast to them, the present study employs a linguistic-rhetorical analysis. Neoclassical criticism is seen as evolving from traditional Rhetoric which continued from the Middle Ages right up to the eighteenth century. This criticism reaches its climax in the age of Johnson when the critic will assert his autonomy both from Scholastic Rhetoric and from Aristotelian Poetics.

It is only when the rules of criticism are brought down from the *a priori* to the experimental and the direct observation of aesthetic experience and emotional effects, that the road will be open for Romantic criticism: which will bring to their logical conclusion the implications of the revolt against all past authority and prescriptive rules of writing and of criticism alike.

Department of English
University of Haifa

SASCHA TALMOR

Acknowledgements

Chapter 5, section b has appeared in an expanded version under the title "Fancy and Imagination in Coleridge's Poetics" in *Durham University Journal*, Vol. LXXIV 2, June 1982. Chapter 3, "A Forgotten Classic: Hume's 'Of the Standard of Taste'" was originally presented at the XVth World Congress of Philosophy at Varna, Bulgaria, September 1973. It has appeared under its title in *Durham University Journal*, Vol. LXXV 1, December 1982.

Contents

Introduction

The problem of the suitability and effectiveness of language, or of man's power of communication with his fellow men, or, in one word, his power of rhetoric, has always been a very complex and elusive problem to formulate and analyse.

Just as there are changes — if not evolution — in different human techniques, I shall assume that rhetoric, or the technique of using language, also changes from period to period, the length of the period itself being variable. (For instance, whereas in the Middle Ages this period lasted for a thousand years, the last fifty years of the twentieth century have seen more changes than the last two centuries.)

Between periods of relative stability and periods of rapid change there are also periods we call transitional, i.e. periods when the old traditional techniques are still adhered to, but when men have already begun to grow dissatisfied with these old, accepted, established or institutionalised ways of action, behaviour, speech and writing. Their dissatisfaction or even outright rejection of the old ways finds expression in all spheres of human activity — the moral, religious, social, political, intellectual and personal spheres.

This criticism of, and dissatisfaction with, the old and the search for new ways, practices and techniques is itself accompanied by a secondary rhetorical technique which introduces new realms or levels of effectiveness and suitability. (When I exhort, describe, narrate, tell or show, I am engaged in a first-order rhetorical or linguistic activity; but when I assess or criticise a writer, dramatist or critic, I am engaged in a second-order activity.) The criticism of the old techniques and the advocacy of new ones is therefore a second-order activity (i.e. it is the use of a certain kind of language in order to talk about language), which makes the whole problem even more elusive, more difficult to grasp and formulate. The people who are engaged in this activity — critics, philosophers, moralists, preachers — then have recourse to new realms or levels of reality in order to compare and contrast the different techniques of language or the different rhetorics. Whenever we talk about language with regard to its comparative effectiveness, we are in fact talking about rhetoric.

But when talking of linguistic technique or rhetoric, we are not referring
only to stylistic rhetoric: to identify the two is to reduce the effectiveness, import and pervasiveness of language. To reduce the power of language
to the mechanical level of the use of tropes, figures and metaphors is to
distort its very nature. When a technique is applied mechanically it
becomes an obstacle to further development and those who use it become the
slaves of their own techniques: the poet calls them "mind-forged manacles"
and we call them language-forged manacles. No wonder, therefore, that, in
order to break free from the manacles of such a mechanical, routine,
ingrained technique, those people who want to speak and write differently,
as well as those who criticise the accepted way of speaking and writing,
both *appear to* have recourse to different realms of "reality" — psychological, moral and ontological — when, in fact, they are only exploring new
ways of expression more adapted to their own different needs.

The so-called different critical approaches to literature — the moral,
psychological and ontological — derive from a logical or linguistic fallacy.
We do not have three different realms or levels of reality with which the
artist deals in his work, we only have three different ways of talking,
writing about and criticising his work. When Hobbes, in his *Answer to
Davenant*, criticises his contemporaries for using supernatural fictions like
Muses, impenetrable armours, enchanted castles, invulnerable bodies, iron
men, flying horses etc., in their poems, and praises Davenant for dispensing
with these improbable fictions in his epic poem *Gondibert*, he is in fact
advocating a new kind of rhetoric, i.e. a language which is suitable to the
kind of reality which he himself, Davenant and other seventeenth-century
writers believe to be "the true reality". In the twentieth century novelists
and critics will do exactly the same. Thus, for example, Virginia Woolf, in
her famous critical essay "Modern Fiction", criticises her immediate predecessors and contemporaries, the Edwardian and Georgian novelists, for
letting "life" escape them: "Whether we call it life or spirit, truth or
reality, this, the essential thing, has moved off, or on, and refuses to be
contained any longer in such ill-fitting vestments as we provide", she
argues.[1] By choosing to write differently from them, by choosing new and
more fitting vestments, she will try to catch life or truth or "reality".
Just like Hobbes, Virginia Woolf too is dealing with the language of
literature, but is appealing for support to her conception of "reality", i.e.
to the ontological level.

To talk about the "reality" or the "life" captured by, or escaping from, a
specific literary language is an *oblique manner* of talking about its pervasiveness or non-pervasiveness, i.e. its success or failure to fit the
various human practices or the languages concomitant to them.

In the case of such a critic as Coleridge, it is to a different level that
he is referring, or rather seems to be referring, namely, the psychological
level. As I shall show in the sequel, when Coleridge is talking about the
faculties of fancy and imagination in general and of poetic or creative
imagination in particular, he is really arguing in favour of a new poetic
language and technique which is to replace the older, no longer adequate
neoclassical language of poetry and criticism. He is defending his own and
Wordsworth's new poetic language and techniques, no longer fettered by neoclassical forms and canons. We shall see that in his praise of
Shakespeare's, Milton's and Wordsworth's great imagination and his dispraise
of Cowley's and Southey's fancy, Coleridge is really comparing and contrasting their different poetic styles, i.e. their different kinds of rhetoric.
In sum, while seeming to be doing psychological criticism, he was in fact
doing rhetorical or textual criticism of a twentieth-century kind.

In conclusion: a technique is a practice evolved by men in society in order to satisfy their different physical, mental and emotional needs. This technique is all-pervasive, i.e. it informs all human activities. In order to talk about such an all-pervasive technique, men have recourse to a new linguistic or rhetorical device: they split language into different kinds or levels. Thus we get the moral, psychological and ontological levels. If the language used by the poet and critic is regarded as springing from his own mind, his own "mental faculties", then we get what is called psychological criticism; which, as I have pointed out, is a second-order rhetorical technique for dealing with the first-order rhetoric of the poet and critic or of the poetry and criticism.

If the language used by the poet is regarded as having its origin in the language used in and by his society, community or group, and is in accordance with its general rules of speaking, acting and writing, then we get what is called moral criticism. And finally, when the all-pervasiveness is translated into a general theory of reality or being, we get what is called ontological or philosophical criticism. For example, Virginia Woolf's questions: "Is life like this?" "Must novels be like this?" And her answer: "Look within and life, it seems, is very far from being 'like this'.... Life is not a series of of gig-lamps symmetrically arranged; life is a luminous halo, a semi-transparent envelope surrounding us from the beginning of consciousness to the end. Is it not the task of the novelist to convey this varying, this unknown and uncircumscribed spirit, whatever aberration or complexity it may display, with as little mixture of the alien and external as possible?"[2]

It is Hume who must have the last word on this question of reality and our talk about it. Be it noted, however, that Hume does not only speak of "reality" but of "realities". In Book I of *A Treatise of Human Nature*, "Of the Understanding", he writes that there are two kinds of systems which we call realities or existences: "The first of these systems is the object of the memory and the senses; the second of the judgment." We form our present and past impressions, perceptions and memories into a kind of perceptual system which "we are pleased to call a *reality*". But this reality is less important than the second system of reality connected by custom, by the relation of cause and effect or by any experimental reasoning. Such a reality lies beyond the reach of senses and memory: "By means of it I paint the universe in my imagination, and fix my attention on any part of it I please. I form an idea of *ROME*, which I neither see nor remember; but which is connected with such impressions as I remember to have received from the conversation and books of travellers and historians.... All this, and everything else, which I believe, are nothing but ideas; tho' by their force and settled order, arising from custom and the relation of cause and effect, they distinguish themselves from other ideas, which are merely the offspring of the imagination" (*Treatise*, p. 108).

REFERENCES

1. Virginia Woolf, *The Common Reader: First Series* (1925; London: The Hogarth Press, 1968), p. 188.
2. Ibid., p. 189.

PART I

The Seventeenth Century: The Legacy of Rhetoric

"It would be difficult to find another classical work whose importance for Hobbes's political philosophy can be compared with that of the *Rhetoric* [of Aristotle]. The central chapters of Hobbes's anthropology, those chapters on which, more than on anything else he wrote, his fame as a stylist and as one who knows men rests for all time, betray in style and contents that the author was a zealous reader, not to say a disciple of the *Rhetoric*."

(Leo Strauss, *The Political Philosophy of Hobbes*).

CHAPTER 1

The Philosopher as Critic: Hobbes's Rhetorical Criticism

(a) The Answer to Davenant

I

Thomas Hobbes was not only a philosopher but also a man of letters, whose interest in literature and poetry began when he was a student and lasted all his life. His last works, we remember, were translations of Homer's *Iliad* (1673) and *Odyssey* (1675), which he undertook at the age of eighty, because, as he tells us, "I had nothing else to do." After his death he was described as "a great critic and poet" by Anthony à Wood,[1] and Dryden, lovingly calling him "our poet and philosopher of Malmesbury", compared him to the philosopher-poet, Lucretius.[2]

As a man of letters of the old style, Hobbes took all the Republic of Letters for his province. History, philosophy, mathematics, logic, rhetoric, poetry, politics and ethics were his subjects and, as his writings attest, he dealt with each one of them in turn. But, even when he is dealing with a purely literary subject as in his two critical essays, the *Answer to Davenant* (1650)[3] and the *Preface to Homer* (1675),[4] his essential philosophy informs them, just as it informs all he wrote. As a matter of fact, when reading Hobbes's translation of *Thucydides* (1628) — still considered as one of the best — we realise that for Hobbes history, poetry and philosophy are but three different ways of describing, representing and exploring the same subject, namely, human nature itself. And what Hobbes says of the greatness of Thucydides the historian can be applied, *pari passu*, to the poet:

> Thucydides is one, who, though he never digress to read a Lecture, Moral or Political, upon his own Text, nor enter into men's hearts, *further than the Actions themselves evidently guide him*, is yet accounted the most Politick Historiographer what ever writ. The reason whereof I take to be this: He filleth his Narrations with that *choice of matter, and ordereth them with that Judgment, and with such perspicuity and efficacy expresseth himself* that (as Plutarch saith) he maketh his Auditor a Spectator. For he setteth his Reader in the Assemblies of the People, and in the Senates, at their debating; in the Streets, at their Seditions; and in the Field, at their Battels.[5]

3

The subject of the historian then is human nature itself, as it is expressed in military and political action; of the poet and the philosopher, it is human nature too, but as expressed in the whole of man's life, which is, as Aristotle said, action or doing. In our examination of the *Answer to Davenant*, we will see that what Hobbes considers the essential qualities of a great historian are the same as those of a great poet.

Although modern commentators hold the view that Hobbes's literary criticism is theoretical rather than practical, this seems to me mistaken: and we shall see in the sequel that Hobbes never makes pronouncements on the nature of poetry in the void, but immediately goes on to apply them to the matter under consideration, in this case the qualities of the epic poem *Gondibert*. Moreover, for a philosopher like Hobbes, the separation of theory and practice would be unthinkable.

This close connection between theory and practice in Hobbes's philosophy, although apparent in all his works, is best seen in chapter 1 of his *De Corpore*. There Hobbes gives a definition of philosophy, its elements, scope and utility. It is interesting to note that Hobbes regards sense and memory as identical with knowledge, and experience as "nothing but memory".[6] But what is of even greater interest to us is Hobbes's view of the end or scope of philosophy, which is action or practice. As he puts it: "The *end* or *scope* of philosophy is, that we may make use to our benefit of effects formerly seen; or that, by application of bodies to one another, we may produce the like effects of those we conceive in our mind, as far forth as matter, strength, and industry, will permit, for the commodity of human life." And he concludes the passage by again repeating that "The end of knowledge is power; and the use of theorems ... is for the construction of problems; and, lastly, *the scope of all speculation is the performing of some action, or thing to be done.*"[7]

Hobbes's view that the end of philosophy and of all speculation is action, or things to be done for the benefit of man and of mankind — in one word, that the end of thought is practice — is also applicable to that part of philosophy which deals with works of art, i.e. literary criticism. Now it is clear that in his two critical essays Hobbes is doing criticism not for the sake of mere speculation or ratiocination, but for a very practical end: he wants his readers to know what the defining properties of an epic poem are, so that they can then apply this knowledge themselves, for instance to Davenant's epic poem *Gondibert*, or to the works of Homer, Virgil and Lucan. In no case does Hobbes simply enounce a literary principle or rule of art without immediately applying it to a concrete work with the question: Does this poem, or does it not, possess this quality, characteristic or virtue? Is this hero a proper epic hero, i.e. does he or doesn't he possess those qualities we have found by experience to be necessary for such a hero, in such a situation? Is the language of the poem appropriate to the dramatic action, the heroes, the situation, the time and place portrayed? and so forth.

In short, all Hobbes's literary critical determinations, pronouncements and rules are generalisations from experience, based on his reading of literary works and his knowledge of human nature and life; and these generalisations can, in turn, be applied to other works, thus helping the reader to greater understanding and enjoyment. In one word, Hobbes's aim is not speculation or theory, but literary and critical practice.

Finally, one of Hobbes's basic assumptions is that even the successful mastering of some difficult and doubtful matter, or the discovery of some hidden truth, are not worth the difficulties entailed by the study of philosophy. Thus he insists that, for instance, teaching others for the sake of teaching is not enough.[8] For teaching is not an end in itself, but only a means to a practical end, i.e. the performing of some action. In sum, one of the distinctive things about Hobbes is his view that the end of all teaching, thinking and knowledge is practice.

II

What is the logical groundwork of the essay? What method of presentation and argument does it follow? Although the essay itself is not subdivided into different parts, I propose to examine it under the following four headings: (1) *poesis* (poetry in general), (2) *poema* (the epic poem in particular), (3) *poeta* (the qualifications of the poet), and (4) *language*, style or expression.

(1) Poesis or Poetry in General

Hobbes begins by commending *Gondibert* in general terms — its subject matter, structure, characters and expression. The poem is good because Davenant has the necessary qualities of a poet, viz. experience, memory, judgement and a controlled fancy. He adds that he isn't really qualified to judge a poem, not being a poet himself — the implication being that the function and qualifications of a poet are different from those of a philosopher. But then Hobbes immediately tells us what, as a philosopher, he *is* able to do, namely, to analyse "the Nature and differences of Poesy" (p. 54). We shall see in the sequel that the greatest part of the essay is devoted to an analysis of the proper language of poetry.

Already in this introductory passage, Hobbes makes an important point, i.e. the separation of the poet from the philosopher. It is worth recalling at this point that a separate discipline called Criticism did not exist as yet in the seventeenth century; up to the middle of the century, philosophers like Francis Bacon, or poets like Ben Jonson, had dealt with literary theory as part either of general philosophy, or, in the case of Jonson, as some occasional pieces (*Timber* or *Discoveries*),[9] which did not qualify as full-fledged critical treatises. Most writers on critical matters were not just and only critics, they were either philosophers or poets. Criticism was only just beginning to emerge from the general field of letters, with a separate function, method and terminology of its own. It was only Dryden, who, by the end of the eighteenth century, was first given the title of critic when Johnson called him "the father of English criticism".[10]

Whereas the philosophers take the whole universe for their Province, the poets take the world for theirs. By this Hobbes really means not the physical world or the world of nature, but the social world. Seeing that society, or rather English society, can be divided into the court, the city and the country, with its corresponding classes — the aristocracy, the *bourgeoisie* and the peasantry — Hobbes similarly divides poetry into three corresponding kinds, i.e. the heroic, the comic and the pastoral. Such a division of poetry according to social classes and ways of life can be described as materialistic or, at least, as sociological. It is, at all events, an original division, never made by other writers before Hobbes.

Hobbes then goes on and states the end of poetry which is "by imitating humane life in delightful and measur'd lines, to avert men from vice and incline them to vertuous and honorable actions" (pp. 54-55). This is the

accepted view of the end or function of poetry, current during the
Renaissance and the Augustan age. It had been forcefully advocated by
Sidney, who accepted the Horatian dictum that the end of poetry is to teach
and delight. In addition, Hobbes also accepts the traditional Aristotelian
view that poetry is imitation. But the last part of the sentence, "to avert
men from vice and incline them to vertuous and honorable actions", is, of
course, the religious, moral and didactic addition of the Christian
Renaissance, which could not accept the classical view of poetry — best
represented by Aristotle's *Poetics* — as being only pleasure, albeit
pleasure of a special kind.

Having defined the end of poetry, Hobbes then turns to its subject matter.
It is, he writes, "the manners of men, not natural causes; manners presented,
not dictated; and manners feigned, not found in men" (p. 56). This is an
important pronouncement, based on a series of antitheses, by means of which
Hobbes contrasts poetry to natural philosophy, ethics and history.

The natural philosopher deals with natural causes and effects; the poet
deals with men, their behaviour, actions and manners; moreover, in contrast
to the moral philosopher, teacher or preacher, the poet does not prescribe
how men ought to act, he only presents them as acting in certain ways; and
finally, these manners or ways of acting are imagined, they are created by
the poet and then projected into the poem. Whereas the historian cannot
depart from historical facts, and must therefore show us human nature as it
is and men as they really act in war and peace, i.e. how they express their
nature in political and social action, the poet imagines his characters as
being of a certain kind and therefore as acting in a certain way, which is
not actually or factually or historically true. Its truth is of a different
kind altogether, which we might call poetic or imaginative truth. Nevertheless, poets, philosophers and historians all use language in order to paint
their different pictures of human nature.

Hobbes's comparison and contrast between the poet, the philosopher and the
historian has a long literary history. Aristotle was of course the first
to make it in the *Poetics*, and he was followed by all later critics,
especially Sidney, who, in *An Apology for Poetry*, raised the poet above both
the historian and the philosopher, as being more capable of creating a
golden or ideally good and beautiful world than either.[11] The poet then
presents his characters' actions. But, just as the characters themselves
are not real men but only fictions, in the same way their actions are not
real, but "feigned", fictitious or imaginative creations.

But what kind of characters are they? What class do they belong to? And
for whom do they present these exemplary models of behaviour to follow?

Although the end of poetry is the portrayal of the manners of men, the
different kinds or genres of poetry will differ in two ways: first, in the
manner of their presentation, and second, in the sort of men, actions and
manners portrayed. In his division of poetry into narrative and dramatic,
and in its further division into epic, tragedy, satire, comedy, pastoral
(or bucolic) and pastoral comedy, Hobbes follows more or less Aristotle's
main divisions. He excludes didactic or descriptive verse (sonnets, epigrams, eclogues and the like), just as Aristotle had done, because the end
of poetry is neither natural science nor moral teaching.

But it is when he comes to deal with his main subject, namely heroic
poetry, that Hobbes makes his most interesting contributions to literary
theory.

(2) Poema: Heroic or Epic Poetry

We wouldn't do Hobbes justice were we to separate his literary theory from
his general philosophy, especially his political philosophy. The latter is
clearly evident not only in his view of the social hierarchy (court, city
and country), but also in the way this political view determines his
criticism.

The subject of heroic or epic poetry is, Hobbes tells us, "the description
of Great men and Great actions" and of "worthy circumstances" (p. 62). By
"great men" he means what the ancients called heroes, men exalted above
others both by their birth or status, but also — and this is much more
important — by those special qualities of mind and character which would
make them serve as exemplary patterns of behaviour, worthy of imitation. As
Hobbes puts it, "For there is in Princes and men of conspicuous power,
anciently called Heroes, a lustre and influence upon the rest of men resem-
bling that of the Heavens" (p. 55). Moreover, since the purpose of an
heroic poem is to give a noble image of heroic virtue, it is necessary to
inquire what exactly he means by this. In order to do so, we have to look
outside the essay to Hobbes's other works, where "valour, beauty, and love"
and "prudence, justice, and fortitude" are called heroic virtues.[12]

It is clear that Hobbes has a very high ideal of the truly heroic man. It
is an ideal much more encompassing than that of the ancient epic hero, since
love and justice are later Christian moral virtues. And if we ask from
where Hobbes had derived his high ideal of virtue, the answer is not from
the books he had read, but from the experience of his own life. Some
scholars[13] have recently drawn attention to the close group of friends to
which Hobbes belonged, and which used to meet before the Civil War at
Falkland's house at Great Tew. They included Falkland, his good
friend Davenant and Sidney Godolphin the poet, in whom Hobbes seems to have
found his ideal of a "generous nature". This is the social and intellectual
milieu from which sprang Hobbes's refined heroic code, a code to which the
whole group adhered. It was a code modelled on neither the actual moral
code of the aristocracy (based as it was on rank and militarism), nor on
that of any other class. This code whose highest values were courage and
personal relationships was based not on birth or wealth, but on merit —
both moral and intellectual.

This new ideal of a "generous nature" Hobbes found embodied in his friend
Sidney Godolphin, whom he describes as having all the necessary moral and
intellectual qualities: "clearness of judgment, and largeness of fancy;
strength of reason, and graceful elocution; a courage for the war, and a
fear for the laws".[14] And we find a very similar list of virtues in the
essay itself, in Hobbes's generous praise of his friend Davenant in whose
poem he sees "nothing but setled Valor, cleane Honor, calm Counsel,
learned diversion, and pure Love, save onely a torrent or two of Ambition,
which, though a fault, has somewhat Heroick in it, and therefore must have
place in an Heroick Poem" (p. 61).

Ambition then, as Hobbes tells us, although a moral fault, is a heroic
fault, and has therefore its place in a poem describing great men and their
actions. For, as is implied, only great men feel ambition, the majority of
men, as Hobbes says elsewhere, being too busy with getting their livelihood.
Ambition is the last infirmity of noble minds, and the epic which gives an
image of noble minds must portray their natural infirmities as well.

But Hobbes draws the line here: the epic poet, he states, should not portray

what is improper (he calls it "indecent") or really immoral. There are two
kinds of "indecencies" which are absolutely to be avoided: "those that shew
either disproportion between the persons and their actions, or between the
manners of the Poet and the Poem" (p. 64). The first kind are the most
important and refer to the moral character of the heroes, the second to
their language. The poet should avoid "the uncomeliness of representing in
great persons the inhumane vice of Cruelty or the sordid vice of Lust and
Drunkenness" (p. 64).

When Hobbes makes this demand, we realise how mistaken are those of his
modern interpreters who believe him to favour a poetry that is realistic or
exactly true to life as it is. Hobbes was aware that in real life men of
rank, just like other men, are sometimes cruel, sensual and drunk. But he
believed that the poet is to exhibit a high image of virtue and therefore
his heroes had to be purer, nobler and larger than life.

Thus, for example, Hobbes praises Davenant for having painted in his epic
"every excellent picture of virtue", and singles out as a model of excellent
virtue Birtha, the heroine of *Gondibert*. He believes that neither ancient
nor modern poets have succeeded like Davenant to "draw so true, perfect, and
natural a Love to the Life, and make use of nothing but pure Lines, without
the help of any of the least uncomely shadow" (p. 61).

This passage is often taken to show Hobbes's theory of verisimilitude.[15]
But this seems to me mistaken. If we read the passage attentively, and keep
in mind some of Hobbes's other pronouncements on what is "natural", we
realise that he regards Birtha as a successful creation, not because she in
any way is modelled on a real person, but because she exemplifies perfect
love, the like of which can never be found in real life. In life, Hobbes
implies, there are always some "uncomely shadows". But when he nevertheless
calls Birtha's love "natural", he presumably means that it is in human
nature to seek and aspire to such a kind of true and perfect love.

Yet it would be wrong to conclude from the foregoing that Hobbes did not
believe that goodness, truth, nobility of mind and action *are* to be found in
real men. Thus, he praises Davenant himself, his good friend, in unambiguous
terms for the purity of his purpose in writing his epic, for having no other
motive in his labour "but to adorn vertue and procure her Lovers, then which
there cannot be a worthier designe, and more becoming noble Poesy" (p. 58).

That Hobbes firmly held to this didactic view of poetry (and painting) is
clearly stated in what is considered the central passage of the essay, and
the one most often quoted. I refer, of course, to the passage beginning with
"Time and Education begets experience ...", but I shall leave its consideration for later. Here suffice it to quote just the last part, the one
dealing with moral virtue. Hobbes says that "He therefore that undertakes an
Heroick Poem, which is to exhibite a venerable & amiable Image of Heroick
vertue, must not only be the Poet, to place & connect, but also the
Philosopher, to furnish and square his matter, that is, to make both Body and
Soul, colour and shadow of his Poem out of his own Store..." (p. 60).

Hobbes ends by praising Davenant for having performed his task well and goes
on to prove it by considering various aspects of *Gondibert*. But what
interests us at the moment is Hobbes's view that every epic poet must not
only be a poet, but also a philosopher, whose task is to teach moral virtue.
Moreover, Hobbes's view that Davenant is not only a poet but also a
philosopher — a fact generally overlooked by modern commentators — is borne
out by what Hobbes writes later, namely that "I have used your Judgment no

less in many things of mine, which coming to light will thereby appear the better" (p. 65).

Not only did Davenant share many of Hobbes's ideas and principles which he openly acknowledged at the beginning of the *Preface to Gondibert*[16] dedicated "to his much Honour'd FRIEND Mr HOBS", "Since you have done me the honour to allow this Poem a daily examination as it was writing," (p. 1), but Hobbes too, as we have noted, respected his friend's judgement and used it in his work. Hobbes's words have generally been seen as mere compliments, not to be taken literally. It would be truer to say that Hobbes, Davenant and their friends the poets Cowley and Waller, meeting and exchanging their ideas at Great Tew before the Civil War, and later during their exile in Paris, *all* contributed their part in the composition of *Gondibert*; similarly, the ideal of virtue it portrayed was one shared by a minority of intellectuals, believing in an aristocracy of merit (moral and intellectual) rather than birth. Furthermore, to regard Davenant's *Preface* and Hobbes's *Answer* only from the purely literary viewpoint, and to examine them only as illustrations of Hobbes's associationist psychology, is to restrict their range and importance to a single aspect (and a doubtful one at that).

Both Davenant's and Hobbes's critical essays have a much wider importance than a purely literary one; their importance is ethical, social and political as well, but, since these different strands are closely connected, it is very difficult to deal with any one of them separately from the rest.

In addition, we shouldn't forget that these poets and philosophers lived in an age of transition, and that therefore we find in their works principles and standards deriving from an older social order which was soon to disappear completely. In the new society that came into being after the violence of the Civil War, the Protectorate, the Restoration and the Bloodless Revolution of 1688, new ethical and political ideals will emerge which will find their expression in new philosophical systems and a new literature, whose main spokesmen will be Locke and Dryden.

Hobbes himself was convinced that literature and poetry not only reflect the religious, ethical, political and social ideas current at a certain place and time, but he also realised that poetry, if it is to fulfil its end of teaching men virtue, must go beyond mere reflection or representation of actuality. It must project not a picture of actual human nature, but a picture of the possible or probable, in the sense used by Aristotle in the *Poetics*, viz. that "it is not the poet's function to describe what has actually happened, but the kinds of thing that might happen, that is, that could happen because they are, in the circumstances, either probable or necessary" (IX. 1).[17] He would, I think, also agree to Aristotle's view that whereas history describes the particular, poetry describes the universal.

(3) Poeta, or the Qualifications of the Poet

It is logical, therefore, for Hobbes to say that "Beyond the actual works of nature a Poet may now go; but beyond the conceived possibilities of nature, never" (p. 62). There are men who want their poetry to be wholly fictitious, exceeding the very possibility of nature, such as "impenetrable Armours, Enchanted Castles, invulnerable bodies, Iron Men, flying Horses, and a thousand such things ..." (p. 61). But what was permissible to the ancient poets like Homer and Virgil, living and writing at a time when men believed in these supernatural fictions, cannot be permitted to a poet

living now. In other words, not only is the ontological commitment — to
use the modern term — of the Greek and English language different, but also
the world picture and the picture of human nature current in ancient and
modern times is different.

In his poetry the poet cannot go "beyond the conceived possibilities of
nature", both physical and human. If he does go beyond it, he simply
portrays an ignorance which is a serious fault in a poet, who must, as
Hobbes says, know well and know much. In order to illustrate his meaning,
Hobbes compares the poet to the geographer; when a geographer paints an
enormous fish or ship in the sea of his map, we accept it as possible; but
when he paints an elephant in the same place, we say it is impossible and
that he is simply ignorant. And the same is true of the poet (pp. 62, 63).

From this point to the end of the essay Hobbes analyses the elements of style
or expression, which, as we shall see, he regards as an integral part of the
substance of the poem.

(4) Language, Style or Expression

All the second part of the essay deals with the proper language or expression of the epic poem. The key word here is "property", decency or proportion: Aristotle called it "propriety" and the Neoclassics will call it
"decorum".

Expression or style, "in which consisteth the countenance and colour of a
beautiful Muse" (p. 62), has two sources: it comes either from the poet
himself, or is borrowed from others. Hobbes clearly prefers the first,
because, presumably, it shows the poet's invention and originality, whereas
the second is mere imitation. When a poet uses his own manner of expression,
based on and revealing his individual experience and knowledge of nature,
especially human nature, we say he has a natural style. But a poet who
models his style on others, i.e. he takes it from books — "the ordinary
boxes of Counterfeit Complexion" (p. 62) — and not from his own experience
and observation, will easily betray his lack of originality, his mere
imitativeness, if his language does not fit his subject. What Hobbes really
means is that there must be coherence between substance and style, content
and form, the body and soul of the poem.

A good style comes from the poet's own experience and knowledge of human
nature. Hobbes enlarges on this further by saying that a good style results
from knowing well and knowing much. To know well means to have distinct and
clear images in the memory and results in perspicuity, propriety of style
and decorum in character drawing; to know much is the source of variety and
novelty of expression which cause wonder, curiosity, delight and desire of
knowledge (p. 63).

What Hobbes really means is that the great poet is recognised by his command
of language, a command that is clearly gained by practice and observation.
Although he seems to start from the poet (i.e. his memory, fancy, imagination,
wit, etc.) and then goes on to the poem (or its language), the real order must
have been different: for Hobbes, no more than anyone else, could know what
happens in a poet's mind or memory when composing a poem. It is only because
a certain poem has distinct and clear images, because its style is varied
and new, because the characters are well differentiated by means of their
different ways of expression, that Hobbes — and all readers for that
matter — can make certain inferences regarding the mind of the poet.

It should be observed at this point, however, that my view and interpretation of Hobbes's meaning is radically different from that of all his modern commentators like D. F. Bond,[18] Martin Kallich[19] and C. D. Thorpe, who all assign a major place to Hobbes's psychology and theory of the imagination. Thorpe, for instance, expresses the current view when he states that, "in order to understand Hobbes's theory of the imagination, or, more broadly, the creative process, it is necessary to know the psychology upon which this theory rests: in other words that we must first find Hobbes's ideas of the make-up of the poet's mind before we can understand how that mind can and does work in poetic creation."[20]

I wish to contend this view: Hobbes was not interested in "the make-up of the poet's mind", any more than he was in the way that mind works in poetic creation. But he was interested in the finished product of that mind, i.e. in the poem itself. And as such, Hobbes belongs to the traditional classical school of critics who regarded the examination of all forms of discourse to be their proper task.

When saying, therefore, that Homer, or Virgil, or Davenant, know human nature well and know much about it, what one really means is that the fictional characters created by these poets are convincing, are individualised, are life-like, are natural. And this can be achieved only be means of a clear, natural, transparent language, what Hobbes calls a "natural contexture of words": "For the order of words, when placed as they ought to be, carries a light before it, whereby a man may foresee the length of the period, as a torch in the night shews a man the stops and unevenness in the way. But when plac'd unnaturally, the Reader will often find unexpected checks, and be forced to go back and hunt for the sense, and suffer such unease, as in a coach a man unexpectedly finds in passing over a furrow" (p. 69).

Although this quotation comes from a later essay, The *Preface to Homer (1675) or The Virtues of an Heroic Poem*, it is relevant here, in our examination of the language of epic poetry. In this beautiful metaphor of language as a lighted torch, showing the reader his way (and the related implicit metaphor of an unnatural order of words as a badly placed light which prevents him from seeing his way), Hobbes emphasises the great importance he gives to natural expression. Only a poet whose language lights the reader's way before him, so that he can confidently see where it is leading him and where he is going, without having to hunt for the sense, and without having to stop because of unexpected obstacles on his way, only such a poet will qualify as good or great.

Although a natural expression is the first requirement of a poet, Hobbes knows that naturalness alone is not enough. Poetic language uses imagery, i.e. metaphors and similes. But, just as there is a proper or improper order of words, there are good and bad metaphors and similes. Here again the good poet is he whose imagery is varied, new and apt:

> From *Knowing much*, proceedeth the admirable variety and novelty of Metaphors and Similitudes, which are not possible to be lighted on in the compass of a narrow knowledge. And the want whereof compelleth a Writer to expressions that are either defac'd by time or sullied with vulgar or long use. For the Phrases of Poesy, as the airs of musick, with often hearing become insipide, the Reader having no more sense of their force than our Flesh is sensible of the bones that *sustain it. As the sense we have of bodies consisteth in change and variety of*

impressions, so also does the sense of language in the variety and changeable use of words. I mean not in the affectation of words newly brought home from travail, but in new and with all significant translation to our purposes of those that be already received, and in far fetch'd but withal apt, instructive, and comly similitudes" (p. 65, my italics).

This is an important and very beautiful passage, whose central statement I have italicised. Hobbes first of all contrasts knowing much with knowing little. But what becomes clear to us in the very next lines is that Hobbes does not here refer to knowledge in general, to abstract knowledge of philosophy, ethics, logic or science, but to a very specific and concrete knowledge — the knowledge of language. It is from a wide and thorough knowledge of language that the poet draws the variety and novelty of his metaphors and similes. The minor or bad poet is recognised by his lack of a varied or original style; he is simply reduced to using what other poets have used before him, to the repetition of familiar metaphors and similes which have become boring and hackneyed. Certain Augustan images of this kind immediately come to mind — "the finny tribe", "the cooling western breeze", "whispers thro' the trees", etc. The hackneyed phrase, the cliché, the insipid and vulgar words are all censured because they prove the poet's lack of mastery of his art, his narrow knowledge of language.

Hobbes, just as Aristotle before him, knew that for a poet "the most important thing to master is the use of metaphor". He would most probably also have subscribed to Aristotle's saying, that "This is the one thing that cannot be learnt from anyone else, and it is the mark of great natural ability, for the ability to use metaphor well implies a perception of resemblances" (*Poetics*, XXII. 5).[21]

What Aristotle calls "great natural ability", Hobbes calls "the excellency of *fancy*" from which "proceed those grateful similes, metaphors and other tropes by which both *poets* and *orators* have it in their power to make things please or displease...." An excellent fancy or "*quick ranging* of mind" is the ability of "finding unexpected *similitude* of things otherwise unlike ... or else in discerning suddenly *dissimilitude* in things that otherwise appear the same."[22]

It is clear from the foregoing that for both Aristotle and Hobbes, a poet's great intellectual ability is seen in his command of language, and, moreover, in that most important element of language which reveals creative imagination — metaphor. It is by means of his mastery of metaphor that the poet shows insight: when once he has shown us the similarity between different things and the difference between similar things through telling and appropriate metaphors, he has helped us see what we couldn't see before. He has increased our knowledge of reality by means of his language. It is a commonplace of modern criticism that Shakespeare's greatness consists neither in his ideas, nor in his philosophy of life, but in his extraordinary command of language. It is not what Shakespeare tells us that is important, but what his imagery tells us.

The kind of metaphor Hobbes has in mind as a mark of the poet's ability is not metaphor-as-ornament but metaphor-as-insight, and this we have seen in the passage cited above. There is no doubt that for Hobbes vivid imagery was important, the sign of an alert mind, just as a poor language was the sign of dullness. In his very first published work, *The Whole Art of Rhetoric* (1637 [?]), Hobbes writes: "But *metaphors* please; for they beget in us, by the *genus*, or by some *common* things to that with another, a kind of *science*. As when an *old man* is called *stubble*; a man suddenly learns that he grows up, flourisheth, and withers like grass, being put in mind of it by the qualities common to *stubble* and to *old men*.

"That which a *metaphor* does, a *similitude* does the same; but with less *grace*, because with more *prolixity*" (*English Works*, III, ix).[23]

The key phrase in this passage is "a man suddenly learns that ...". Because the mark of a good metaphor is that it does give us sudden insight, that we see the thing in a flash and exclaim, Yes, the poet is right, this is so! We describe our feeling or aesthetic experience by such words as insight, revelation, intuition, illumination or heightened awareness. Hobbes simply calls it "science".

What is for the poet a way of perceiving similar or dissimilar objects will become for us, the readers, a way of looking at them. When the metaphor or simile is good, apt, appropriate, right, then we come to see the things before our eyes. As Hobbes puts it in a later passage: *"Animation is that expression which makes us seem to see the thing before our eyes. As he that said, The Athenians poured out their city into Sicily*; meaning, they sent hither the greatest army they could make."[24]

We have seen that for Hobbes the good poet is capable of producing new and varied metaphors and similes. But he warns against the use of words that are so new and strange as to be completely unfamiliar, what Hobbes calls "the affectation of words newly brought home from travail", by which he presumably means the learned words of erudite poets, which seem affected and unnatural. Good metaphors should be neither too familiar or common, nor too far-fetched. Hobbes's ideal metaphor is the mean between the too familiar and the too unfamiliar; as he writes at the end of the paragraph, the poet should use "far fetch'd but withal apt, instructive, and comly similitudes".

In the most important line of the passage, Hobbes compares language to bodies or objects, and says that, just as the sense we have of bodies (or objects) consists in the change and variety of our impressions we receive from them, so does the sense of language consist in the variety and changeable use of words. We have already encountered a similar comparison of language to a living organism in Horace, who compared it to a wood, continually shedding its old dry leaves and putting forth new ones.[25] Hobbes similarly sees language not as something fixed and rigid, but living, changing, growing and also decaying.

Hobbes censures the use of learned words taught in the Schools, just as he dislikes "strong lines" or metaphysical conceits. He censures the former because, as he says, "There be so many words in use at this day in the English Tongue, that though of magnifique sound, yet (like the windy blisters of a troubled water) have no sense at all, and so many others that lose their meaning by being ill coupled, that it is a hard matter to avoid them; for having been obtruded upon youth in the Schools by such as make it, I think, their business there (as 'tis exprest by the best Poet)

With terms to charm the weak and pose the wise,

they grow up with them, and, gaining reputation with the ignorant, are not easily shaken off."

And the latter are similarly censured:

"To this palpable darkness I may also add the ambitious obscurity of expressing more than is perfectly conceived, or perfect conception in fewer words than it requires. Which Expressions, though they have had the honor of being called strong lines, are indeed no better than Riddles, and, not onely to the Reader but also after a little time to the Writer himself, dark and troublesome" (p. 63).

We see here Hobbes's strong dislike of the erudite language of the Schools and the exaggerated obscurity of metaphysical conceits. Words and thoughts should fit each other, Hobbes implies, words neither expressing more nor less than the corresponding thoughts. Obscurity of language (and thought) is just as bad as a too concentrated language, which prevents the reader from understanding the meaning of the words used, and hence prevents him from "seeing" the objects described.

Hobbes, we realise, is arguing for a close correspondence of words and thoughts, and perhaps also of words and things. His dislike of loan words and scholarly coinages, of far-fetched metaphysical conceits and virtuosity for its own sake, of technical terms and words drawn from "humble or evil Arts" in an epic poem, show his purism: the best style is clear and natural. Hobbes's severe criticism of a flowery, bombastic, inflated and artificial style foreshadows the kind of style which will come into favour in the eighteenth century. But in his own time, it is probably best exemplified in his own work.

We have already examined most of the points raised in the essay. Now we are ready to examine the last and most important passage, namely the well-known and oft-quoted passage:

> Time and Education begets experience; Experience begets memory; Memory begets Judgment and Fancy: Judgment begets the strength and structure, and Fancy begets the ornaments of a Poem. The Ancients therefore fabled not absurdly in making memory the Mother of the Muses. For Memory is the World (though not really, yet so as in a looking glass) in which the Judgment, the severer Sister, busieth her self in a grave and rigid examination of all the parts of Nature, and in registering by Letters their order, causes, uses, differences, and resemblances; Whereby the Fancy, when any work of Art is to be performed, findes her materials at hand and prepared for use, and needs no more then a swift motion over them, that what she wants, and is there to be had, may not lie too long unespied. So that when she seemeth to fly from one *Indies* to the other, and from Heaven to Earth, and to penetrate into the hardest matter and obscurest places, into the future and into her self, and all this in a point of time, the voyage is not very great, her self being all she seeks; and her wonderful celerity consisteth not so much in motion as in copious Imagery discreetly ordered & perfectly registred in the memory, which most men under the name of Philosophy have a glimpse of, and is pretended to by many that, grosly mistaking her, embrace contention in her place (pp. 59-60).

Whenever this passage is quoted, it is used as incontrovertible evidence for Hobbes's psychological approach to literature, and, moreover, as a proof of his associationism. This mistaken view seems to me to arise from a confusion between the metaphorical language Hobbes uses to describe the creative process and his real intention. I contend that Hobbes's real intention was to describe the literary work, the finished product, and not the mind of the poet when writing the poem. For, if Hobbes's main intention in the essay in general, and in this passage in particular, was really to give us a detailed analysis of the workings of the poet's mind and of the process of poetic creation, how could he expect us to accept both his quasi-mechanical account of the mind as passively reacting to external stimuli *and* his account of the powers of the mind (or of the imagination) as active, originating in the mind itself and carried on within it? I am of course referring to the above-cited lines about fancy "that when she seemeth to fly from one *Indies* to the other, and from Heaven to Earth, ... the voyage is not very great, her self being all she seeks ...".

Furthermore, how could people be taught to be critical by being told of the source of our ideas in memory and imagination, of the compounding of our simple ideas into compound ones, of the different types of "trains of thought" into which they combined, etc? Can ordinary or even highly intelligent people be converted from non-poets into poets, or from non-critics into critics, by examining the mechanics of their own intellectual operations? Why should we think or write or understand or criticise better for knowing the nature, scope and functions of our different mental faculties? Or for knowing how our thoughts cohere into "trains of thought", ideas, images or conceptions? I believe that the answer to these questions is quite simple: we don't.

If this is true, i.e. if we neither think, write, nor criticise better for knowing the mechanics of our intellectual operations, then why did Hobbes trouble to analyse them in the way he did? The answer to this question is not so simple, but seems to me to be the following:

What Hobbes was really trying to do was to give an account of our mental operations and aptitudes in a language that dispenses with such traditional notions as the existence of innate ideas, *a priori* reasoning, divine inspiration, scholastic Universals or essences. In short, he wanted to purify both thought and language of any ungrounded beliefs, superstitions, abstruse and esoteric terms. As Hobbes so directly puts it: "There be so many words in use at this day in the English Tongue, that though of magnifique sound, yet ... have no sense at all, and so many others that lose their meaning by being ill coupled, that it is a hard matter to avoid them; for having been obtruded upon youth in the Schools ... they grow up with them, and, gaining reputation with the ignorant, are not easily shaken off" (p. 63).

In his lifelong polemic against scholasticism and any form of obscurantism, Hobbes repeatedly attacks their doctrines and terminology because they confuse men's minds with metaphysical superstitions. Hobbes then goes on to contend against another "palpable darkness": "To this palpable darkness I may also add the ambitious obscurity of expressing more than is perfectly conceived, or perfect conception in fewer words then it requires. Which Expressions, though they have had the honor to be called strong lines, are indeed no better then Riddles, and, not onely to the Reader but also after a little time to the Writer himself, dark and troublesome" (p. 63).

III

Hobbes's extreme nominalism, i.e. that "thinking is reckoning with words", and his demand for clarity, concreteness and precision of speech, served him well in his sustained fight against all occult, esoteric, metaphysical and scholastic doctrines regarding the nature of thought and the workings of the human mind. In his own philosophy, Hobbes argued that all our ideas of things, just as all poetic creation, spring from our perceptions, memory, observation and experience, i.e. from human *practice*. Similarly, all the purpose of our thoughts, imaginations and creations is again practice, action or the doing of certain things.

As Gilbert Ryle in his essay on "John Locke" has put it, there is a world of difference between our theories about our actions, thoughts, perceptions, memories, resolutions and the rest, and our actions, thoughts, perceptions or resolutions themselves. And the difference lies in "the *purposive* nature of our doings, thinkings, perceivings, etc. In our actions, unlike our mere reactions, either there is success or there is failure, and either dexterity or clumsiness".[26] Moreover, all our actions, even the very simplest, must be learned. And the same is true of perception, and finally of thought itself: "Some practice and often some tuition is a *sine qua non* of our being able to think out any problems at all, however simple, within certain fields." And the conclusion is that "In our thinking we exercise good, moderate or bad craftsmanship. Thought is not something that just happens to us and in us, like digestion. It is something that we do, and do well or badly, carefully or carelessly, expertly or amateurishly."[27]

Hobbes, I think, could not agree more. For him too thinking, writing, criticising, arguing, was something that could be done well or badly, expertly or amateurishly. As we have seen, he points out again and again how those who use learned words or words without any definite meaning — especially those of the Schoolmen, the Catholic Church and of medieval psychology — are confusing the ignorant and maintaining their hold on men's minds. And what is true of the Schoolmen, the divines, and the self-professed philosophers, is also true of the poets, or rather the poetasters. They do not do their own thinking, feeling and writing, they simply copy and imitate the thoughts, feelings and writings of other poets. It is here that Hobbes argues so forcefully against imitation in all its aspects. As he puts it:

> That which he (the poet) hath of his own is nothing but experience and knowledge of Nature, and specially humane nature, and is the true and natural Colour. But that which is taken out of Books (the ordinary boxes of Counterfeit Complexion) shews well or ill, as it hath more or less resemblance with the natural, and are not to be used without examination unadvisedly. For in him that professes the imitation of Nature, as all Poets do, what greater fault can there be then to bewray an ignorance of nature in his Poem, -- especially having a liberty allowed him, if he meet with any thing he cannot master, to leave it out? (pp. 62-63).

In Hobbes's insistence on the two qualifications of the poet — knowing much and knowing well — he means that the poet must be an expert craftsman of words, and, moreover, his words must exactly (not approximately) express his meaning. It is only when the poet — just like the philosopher — knows what he wants to say, that he will be able to say it well and clearly. And both the what and the how are skills that the poet must learn, and like other skills, learn by trial and error. As Ryle puts it, "What a person thinks on a certain matter is true or else it is false; it is accurate or else it is inaccurate; it is definite or else it is vague; it is clear or it is muddled; it is well or else ill founded; it is expert or else it is amateurish, and so on."[28] Moreover, how a person expresses what he thinks can also be done accurately or inaccurately; definitely or vaguely; clearly or ambiguously; in one word, well or badly. Thus, not only thinking, but also saying and writing "is a consortium of competences and skills".

In sum, this is exactly what Hobbes was trying to do in his critical essays, both in his *Answer to Davenant* and his later *Preface to Homer*. He did not set out to develop a new theory of the imagination or of the creative process, nor did he proceed to apply his theory of association of ideas or "trains of thought" to an examination of the poet's mind when engaged in poetic creation. What he did do was to examine that special "consortium of skills and competences" required for the writing of poetry, especially epic poetry. And he has convincingly shown us that, just like any other skill, the creation and composition of a work of literature requires learning, knowledge, observation and experience, in one word requires *practice*. Hobbes, therefore, is not a psychological critic, but a practical, rhetorical critic, interested in the how rather than the what of literary production. We saw that for Hobbes "The end of knowledge is power ... and, lastly, the scope of all speculation is the performing of some action, or thing to be done." In the same way, his critical essays are a careful examination and analysis of the *linguistic* skills and competences required for the successful writing of an epic poem.

REFERENCES

1. Anthony à Wood, *Athenae Oxonienses* (London, 1813), Vol. III, p. 1208.
2. "Preface to *Sylvae*" (1685), in *Essays of John Dryden*, ed. W. P. Ker, 2 vols. (New York: Russell & Russell, 1961; 1st ed. 1899), Vol. I, p. 259.
3. Thomas Hobbes, *Answer to Davenant's Preface to Gondibert* (1650), in *Critical Essays of the Seventeenth Century*, ed. J. E. Spingarn, 3 vols. (Bloomington, London: Indiana Univ. Press, 1968; 1st ed. Oxford: Clarendon Press, 1908), Vol. II, pp. 54-67.
4. Thomas Hobbes, *The Preface to Homer* (1675), in Spingarn, op. cit., Vol. II, pp. 67-76. All references to these two essays by Hobbes are to Spingarn, and I will give page numbers in the body of the text.
5. Quoted in Thucydides, *History of the Peloponnesian War*, translated with an Introduction by Rex Warner (Penguin Books, 1954), p. 5 (my italics).
6. Thomas Hobbes, *Body, Man, and Citizen*, edited with an Introduction by Richard S. Peters (New York, N.Y.: Collier Books, 1962), p. 24.
7. Ibid., p. 27 (my italics).
8. Ibid.
9. Ben Jonson, *Timber, or Discoveries* (1620-35?), in Spingarn, Vol. I, pp. 17-64. This is a collection of notes, extracts and reflections on different subjects, varying in length from a single sentence to short essays. They are, for the greater part, adapted from Latin writers.
10. Samuel Johnson, "John Dryden", in *Lives of the English Poets*, Introduction by Arthur Waugh, 2 vols. (London: Oxford Univ. Press, 1973), Vol. I, p. 287.
11. Philip Sidney, *An Apology for Poetry*, in *English Critical Texts*, ed. D. G. Enright and E. De Chickera (London: Oxford Univ. Press, 1962), pp. 14-15.
12. *The English Works of Thomas Hobbes of Malmesbury*, collected and edited by Sir William Molesworth (London: John Bohn, 1840; 2nd rpt. Germany: Scientia Verlag Aalen, 1966), Vol. X, pp. iv, iii. Hereafter cited as *English Works*.
13. See, for example, Keith Thomas, "The Social Origins of Hobbes's Political Thought", in *Hobbes Studies*, ed. K. C. Brown (Oxford: Basil Blackwell, 1965), pp. 185-236.
14. *English Works*, Vol. III, p. 702.
15. C. D. Thorpe, *The Aesthetic Theory of Thomas Hobbes* (New York: Russell & Russell Inc., 1964), p. 159.

16. Sir William Davenant, *Preface to Gondibert*, in *Critical Essays of the Seventeenth Century*, Vol. II, pp. 1-53.

17. Aristotle, *On the Art of Poetry*, in *Classical Literary Criticism*, translated with an Introduction by T. S. Dorsch (Penguin Books, 1965), p. 43.

18. Donald F. Bond, "The Neo-Classical Psychology of the Imagination", *ELH*, iv (1937), 245-264.

19. Martin Kallich, *The Association of Ideas and Critical Theory in Eighteenth-Century England* (The Hague, Paris: Mouton, 1970), pp. 17-34 *et passim*.

20. C. D. Thorpe, op. cit., p. 113.

21. Aristotle, op. cit., p. 65.

22. Thomas Hobbes, *Human Nature*, in *Body, Man, and Citizen*, p. 227.

23. *The Whole Art of Rhetoric*, Vol. III, p. 9, in *English Works*, Vol. VI, p. 496.

24. Ibid., p. 497.

25. Horace, *On the Art of Poetry*, in *Classical Literary Criticism*, p. 81. "As the woods change their foliage with the decline of each year, and the earliest leaves fall, so words die out with old age; and the newly born ones thrive and prosper just like human beings in the vigour of youth."

26. Gilbert Ryle, "John Locke", in *Collected Papers*, Vol. I, Critical Essays (London: Hutchinson & Co. Ltd., 1971), p. 153.

27. Ibid., p. 154.

28. Ibid.

(b) The Preface to Homer

I

Hobbes is often called the father of modern scientific psychology. Starting as he did from a scientific theory of human nature, and applying it to logic, psychology, ethics, politics, law, religion and literature, he came to far-reaching and startlingly modern conclusions in all these fields. In literary criticism, he is generally regarded as the originator of the theory of "association of ideas", which was to become the main literary theory of the eighteenth century, until ousted by the Romantic theory of the Imagination as the source and substance of artistic activity.

Modern commentators are almost unanimous in tracing the psychological theory of criticism to Hobbes.[1] Allowing for minor variations of emphasis, they base their view on the fact that Hobbes assigns an important place to the Imagination or Fancy in his major essay on criticism, the *Answer to Davenant*[2] (1650), written as an answer to Davenant's *Preface to Gondibert* (1650) and dedicated "To his much Honour'd Friend Mr Hobs." In their commentaries these critics also draw on various passages from the *Leviathan* (1651), Hobbes's great philosophical work. Strangely enough, very little attention is paid to the *Preface to Homer*[3] (1675), whose *Odyssey* Hobbes had translated at the age of eighty-five, "Because", as he tells us, "I had nothing else to do" (p. 76).

In the present chapter, I shall challenge the accepted view of Hobbes's theory of poetry and criticism as being the logical result of his theory of the imagination. I shall present Hobbes in a new light, namely as the first English new critic, interested not in the application of an associationist psychology to literature, but in practical, analytical, textual criticism which has become the most widespread critical practice of our time. I shall examine in detail the little-known *Preface to Homer*. It is in this short Preface to his translation of the *Odyssey* that Hobbes reveals himself as a forerunner of modern criticism, both in his language and his method.

ON CONSEQUENCES OF SPEECH

In the *Leviathan*, Part I, Of Man, chapter IX, "Of the Several Subjects of

Knowledge", Hobbes gives a synoptic table to show the divisions of philosophy or science, according to the diversity of subject matter. The table begins with a definition of science: *"Science, that is, Knowledge of Consequences; which is called also Philosophy."* Hobbes then divides the "Consequences from the Qualities of Men in Special" into two parts: (1) Consequences from the Passions, which he calls Ethiques, and (2) Consequences from Speech. Four sciences derive from the consequences of speech: "Poetry, Rhetorique, Logique, and The Science of Just and Unjust."[4]

In classifying poetry, rhetoric, logic and law as consequences of speech, Hobbes speaks directly to the twentieth century, or rather, to those twentieth-century philosophers and critics who regard language as their proper concern. Nevertheless, as I've already noted, modern commentators have labelled Hobbes a psychological critic, whereas, as I shall show in the sequel, he is a nominalist in his theory of language, and a rhetorical critic in his theory of poetry and criticism.

According to Hobbes, therefore, in studying mathematics (arithmetic and geometry) we are studying the consequences of words standing for quantity and motion. In studying meteorology we are studying the consequences of words standing for bodies transient, i.e. that sometimes appear, sometimes vanish. When studying the consequences of words which stand for qualities of vegetables, minerals, stones or metals, we are studying the science of the parts of the earth which are without sense. When studying ethics (or "Ethiques") we are studying the consequences of words which stand for the passions of man (psychology?).

But in studying poetry, rhetoric, logic, and law, we are studying the consequences of speech or the qualities of the words themselves. Generally speaking, in Hobbes's view all philosophy or science starts from right definitions, and proceeds by demonstration to the consequences (what we call the "logical implications") of these same definitions. However, whereas in astronomy and geometry, for example, our words must stand for (or be the marks for) qualities of celestial bodies, or quantities, or motions, in our study of rhetoric, logic or poetry our words stand for the qualities of the words themselves.

The language of poetry is rhetorical or persuasive: its aim is the raising of passion from opinion,[5] not from opinion when judged as true or false (for Hobbes there is no difference between truth and true propositions), but from opinion as reproducing images or "phantasms".[6]

It is this theory of Hobbes which has led many modern commentators to regard him as the originator of psychological criticism. But it is one thing to say, as Hobbes does, that the language of the poet stands for images, and quite another to say, as Thorpe and Kallich do, that the critical criteria deal exclusively, or mainly, with the aptness of that language to evoke passions.

When Hobbes uses such new terms as "images", "passions", "phantasms", and "fancy" in his philosophical and critical writings, he has a very definite and practical aim in view: he simply wants to persuade the poets to use their *own* images, their *own* fancy, their *own* phantasms, their *own* passions, their *own* expressions — in one word, their *own* experience when writing poetry. It is therefore by no means in order to replace the purely rhetorical, linguistic or formal criteria in judging a poem that Hobbes introduces these mental concepts. The so-called "psychologism" in Hobbes's critical theory is *not* a set of criteria for judging a poem, but *a set of*

TABLE OF THE SEVERAL SUBJECTS OF SCIENCE

SCIENCE, that is, knowledge of consequences; which is called also PHILOSOPHY.

- Consequences from the accidents of bodies natural; which is called NATURAL PHILOSOPHY.
  - Consequences from the accidents common to all bodies natural; which are *quantity, and motion*
    - Consequences from quantity, and motion *indeterminate*; which being the principles or first foundation of philosophy, is called *Philosophia Prima*. — **PHILOSOPHIA PRIMA.**
    - Consequences from motion and quantity *determined*.
      - Consequences from quantity, and motion determined.
        - By Figure . . — **GEOMETRY.**
        - By Number . . — **ARITHMETIC.** *(Mathematics)*
      - Consequences from the mot-ion and quantity of the greater parts of the world, as the *earth and stars*. — *Cosmography*
        - Consequences from the mot-ion of the sun and stars — **ASTRONOMY**
        - Consequences from the mot-ion, and quantity of bodies in *special*. — **GEOGRAPHY**
      - Consequences from the motions of special kinds, and figures of body. — *Mechanics.* Doctrine of *weight*. — *Science of* ENGINEERS. ARCHITECTURE. NAVIGATION.
  - PHYSICS or consequences from *qualities*
    - Consequences from the qualities of bodies *transient*, such as sometimes appear, sometimes vanish, *Meteorology*. — **METEOROLOGY.**
    - Consequences from the qualities of bodies *permanent*.
      - Consequences from the qualities of the *stars* .
        - Consequences from the *light* of the stars. Out of this, and the motion of the *sun*, is made the science of . — **SCIOGRAPHY.**
        - Consequences from the *influence* of the stars . — **ASTROLOGY.**
      - Consequences of the qual-ities from *liquid* bodies, that fill the space between the stars; such as are the *air*, or substances ethereal.
      - Consequences from the qualities of bodies ter-restrial.
        - Consequences from the motion of the parts of the earth, that are *without* sense.
          - Consequences from the qualities of *minerals*, as *stones, metals, etc.*
          - Consequences from the qualities of *vegetables*.
        - Consequences from the qualities of *animals*.
          - Consequences from the qualities of *animals in general*.
            - Consequences from *vision* — **OPTICS**
            - Consequences from *sounds* — **MUSIC**
            - Consequences from the rest of the *senses*
          - Consequences from the qualities of *men in special*.
            - Consequences from the *passions* of men . — **ETHICS**
            - Consequences from *speech*.
              - In *magnifying, vilifying, etc.* — **POETRY.**
              - In *persuading,* — **RHETORIC.**
              - In *reasoning,* — **LOGIC.**
              - In *contracting,* — The *Science* of JUST and UNJUST
- Consequences from the accidents of *politic* bodies which is called POLITICS, and CIVIL PHILOSOPHY.
  - 1. Of consequences from the *institution* of COMMONWEALTHS, to the *rights*, and *duties* of the *body politic or sovereign*.
  - 2. Of consequences from the same, to the *duty* and *right* of the *subjects*.

presuppositions which must be fulfilled for a work of art to be called a
work of art. When these presuppositions are fulfilled, e.g. when the poet
has used *his* images, phantasms, fancy and experience, then the critic steps
in and proceeds to evaluate the poem according to rhetorical and formal
criteria appropriate to it.

Had Hobbes really been a psychological critic he would not have classified
criticism ("Poetry") as a science, let alone a science which studies the
consequences of words *qua* words. The fact is that Hobbes *has* classified
criticism with rhetoric, logic and law. We know to what extent Hobbes's
logic was formalistic and linguistic. For him the laws of logic — unlike
the laws of physics — are *arbitrary* definitions: and hence to Hobbes is
attributed the beginning of the conventionalist theory of necessary truths
(logic). In the development of his philosophy, logic is connected with the
doctrine that our thinking is only the manipulation of signs.[7]

We can only conclude that, had Hobbes written a new *Poetics*, it would have
been a purely formal treatise, just like Aristotle's *Poetics*.

II

THE PREFACE TO HOMER

Since poetry, rhetoric, logic and law, or, as Hobbes calls it, "the science
of the just and the unjust", are all consequences of speech or language, it
is natural for Hobbes to devote the greatest part of his critical essays to
a detailed analysis of the language of poetry, i.e. to its rhetorical
devices. This linguistic or rhetorical approach is best seen in the *Preface
to Homer*.

In the Preface concerning *The Vertues of an Heroique Poem*, Hobbes lists the
seven characteristics that concur to make an heroic poem pleasant: "And they
are contained, first, in the choice of words. Secondly, in the construction.
Thirdly, in the contrivance of the Story or Fiction. Fourthly, in the
Elevation of the Fancie. Fifthly, in the Justice and Impartiality of the
Poet. Sixthly, in the clearness of the Descriptions. Seventhly, in the
Amplitude of the Subject" (p. 68).

Hobbes devotes the whole essay to an examination of these seven qualities,
illustrating them by examples drawn from Homer, Virgil and Lucan. It is
worth emphasising that all the seven qualities pertain or refer to language.
Only one, the last, deals with subject matter, but even here Hobbes does not
enlarge on the kind of subject chosen, only on its amplitude or range. One
quality, the fifth, refers to the poet, demanding that he be just and
impartial. This applies to the poet just as to the historian, since both
deal — or should deal — with "matter of fact", i.e. historical facts or
facts of human nature.

The other six qualities all deal with the form or language of the heroic
poem. There is hardly a term in the whole essay that could be said to
belong to psychology (with the only exception of "Fancie"), or to a theory
of poetic creation, or an analysis of the poet's mind in terms of the
association of ideas.

Hobbes gives his full attention to the qualities of the created poem, the
work of art, and doesn't seem at all concerned with questions of psychological processes, inspiration or creation. (The fourth quality is a border-
line case, and, as we shall see in the sequel, it is not easy to state

definitely what Hobbes means by "elevation of fancy.") In short, what Hobbes *is* concerned with are questions of diction, style, imagery, metaphors, comparisons, descriptions, i.e. purely linguistic or stylistic questions.

For Hobbes the best poet is simply the best rhetorician, a skilled user of all the proper verbal devices: in one word, a craftsman of words. It is a view which was soon to pass out of favour. In fact, twenty-five years later we find Dryden in the *Preface to the Fables* (1700) criticising Hobbes for his whole approach to poetry: "Mr. Hobbes", he writes, "begins the praise of Homer where he should have ended it. He tells us that the first beauty of the epic poem consists in diction; that is, in the choice of words, and harmony of numbers."[8]

Just so. As Dryden says, for Hobbes it is good diction that makes a poem good and a poet good. It is by his use of words that the poet will be known. The best poet — Homer — is called best by virtue of his language, his skilful use of tropes and figures, metaphors, similes and descriptions, as well as by the variety of his subject matter and his impartiality in the presentation of his gods and heroes.

(1) Choice of Words

The first quality of the epic poem is the choice of words or, to use its modern term, diction:

> And (to begin with words) the first Indiscretion is, The use of such words as to the Readers of Poesie (which are commonly Persons of the best Quality) are not sufficiently known. For the work of an Heroique Poem is to raise admiration, principally, for three Vertues, Valour, Beauty, and Love; to the reading whereof Women no less than Men have a just pretence, though their skill in Language be not universal. And therefore forein words, till by long use they become vulgar, are unintelligible to them. Also the name of Instruments and Tools of Artificers, and words of Art, though of use in the Schools, are far from being fit to be spoken by a Heroe.... The character of words that become a Heroe are Property and Significance, but without both the malice and lasciviousness of a Satyr (pp. 68-69).

We see that from the very beginning Hobbes's main concern is to find the best means the poet should use for attracting and holding the attention of the reader. Furthermore, as he points out, since the poet addresses himself as much to men as to women, he must bear in mind that women have less skill in language than men. The poet must, therefore, choose his words carefully, so that he be understood by *all* his readers. Hobbes immediately adds the proviso that readers of poetry are generally only persons of the best quality. And it is they who must therefore serve as the standard of judgement.

The end of the heroic poem, he says, is to raise admiration, a term often used in the seventeenth century to distinguish the feelings aroused by tragedy — pity and fear — from those regarded as proper to the epic. The three qualities for which the epic raises the readers' admiration are courage, beauty and love. And it is worth noting that of these three qualities, only two may be regarded as moral — courage and love — whereas beauty is a physical, not a moral, quality. Moreover, whereas in the Greek epics courage was certainly regarded as the most important virtue of the epic hero, love was not. We should recall at this point that, in his *Answer to Davenant*, Hobbes had greatly praised Davenant for his portrayal of a pure perfect love in Birtha, the heroine, noting that the ancient poets had never portrayed love in their epics. Although Hobbes does not say so, it is clear that he realises that women will be specially attracted by the poetic portrayal of beauty and love, and hence his advice that the poet use words that are known and understood by all his readers. It is in his choice of words that the poet's "discretion" will be seen. And this means the same as "discernment, prudence, judgement" (*OED*).

Having posited that the best words for the epic are those that are known and understood by all persons of best quality, Hobbes goes on to enumerate those words which are *not* to be used: foreign words, technical and scholastic terms. Foreign words will be admitted only when, after long use, they have become familiar enough and have lost their air of foreignness. When Hobbes discusses technical and scholastic terms he no longer seems to have the audience in mind, but the nature and character of the epic heroes. The hero, he says, cannot be familiar with words of artisans (instruments and tools of artificers) on the one hand, nor with words of art used by scholars. He is a man of action, and must therefore use such words as are proper to him. The hero may delight in the arts, may even have skill in some of them. But what makes him a hero are qualities of greater import, the moral qualities of courage, nobility and finally of leadership. Drawing as usual on classical models, Hobbes cites Homer to prove his point: both Achilles and Alexander knew to play the guitar. Yet Homer never praises the first or blames the second for his skill in music.

Hobbes concludes the passage by stating that the language of the epic hero must be proper and significant, meaning that it must be appropriate to the social status and dramatic function of the hero. We note here the first signs of what will become important critical terms in the seventeenth and eighteenth centuries, namely, property, propriety or decorum. In sum, it is the purpose and subject matter as well as the audience to which it is addressed that determine the diction of the epic or heroic poem.

(2) Style

After the choice of diction, Hobbes examines the second quality of the heroic poem, i.e. "the Perspicuity and the Facility of Construction", or what "is usually called a good Style" (p. 69). Just as in the first case, he regards that good which is natural. An unnatural, forced or uneven style, forcing the reader to hunt for the sense, is bad. That means that the order of words must be natural, and the reader shouldn't feel the effort that went into the writing. Not only the kind of words used, but also their order, make a style good or bad. Metrical feet and rhymes — the laws of verse — are an artificial constraint imposed on the natural flow of words. But the poet, while obeying the laws of verse, must be as flexible as possible within these self-imposed and conventional limits.

In this passage, just as in the whole essay, Hobbes expounds a stylistic doctrine that became the accepted doctrine of his time. In its preference for the simple unadorned style of writing and oratory, it clearly derives from Aristotle's *Rhetoric*, which, we recall, Hobbes had translated and abridged in 1637.[9] In 1696 a complete English translation of this major work appeared, so that throughout the seventeenth century English scholars, writers and critics became familiar with this classic of persuasive discourse. But Hobbes was the first to introduce this work in an English version to the

public, and, restating Aristotle's ideals of simplicity and naturalness of
style in his own critical essays, made a major contribution to the development of the new seventeenth-century ideal of a simple, unadorned, natural
and clear style in conversation and literature.

Taking the first two qualities of the epic together, i.e. choice of words
and word order, Hobbes finds that Homer, Virgil and Lucan are all excellent
in their own language; though, possibly because of the different nature of
the two languages, Latin seems more majestic than Greek verse. However, he
adds, majesty is not a quality of words but of the mind which pursues a high
and worthy end. All three poets use known words and a natural style. If,
however, their style does not always seem natural, the fault is not in them
but in their faulty translators.

When Hobbes says that majesty is not a quality of words but a quality of
mind, he recalls to us Longinus's famous dictum that sublimity is "the echo
of a great soul", and Quintilian's view that a good orator must be a man of
strong moral character. Throughout the seventeenth and eighteenth centuries
the moral bias in rhetorical education was very important.

(3a) Contrivance or Arrangement

The third quality of the epic poem is the contrivance, arrangement or
structure of the story. Hobbes begins by comparing history and poetry: the
historian, writing in his own person, must keep strictly to the chronologi-
cal time in which the historical events related actually took place; the
poet, however, does not tell the story in his own person, but lets the
fictional characters tell the story. He can therefore change the sequence
of events, so as to arouse and heighten the interest of his readers. Homer,
for example, does not begin the *Iliad* with the elopement of Helen with Paris,
nor does he begin the *Odyssey* with Ulysses' departure from Troy after its
fall. Both these events are related only in the middle of the epics.

Here Hobbes applies to epic poetry what Aristotle had said of tragic poetry,
namely that the poet should start *in medias res*, in the very thick of the
dramatic action.

So far Hobbes clearly means by *contrivance* what classical and Renaissance
critics and rhetoricians had called *arrangement*, i.e. effective ways of
organising the material. (It may be worth recalling at this point that
classical, Renaissance and English rhetoricians of the seventeenth century
were mostly dealing with the Rhetoric of prose, helpful to the politician,
homilist, preacher and essayist. In the second part of the seventeenth
century, when Hobbes was writing his critical essays, there was as yet no
clear distinction between *Rhetoric* and *Poetics*. Their boundaries were in
fact completely blurred, so much so that it would be true to say of many
essays included in Spingarn's three volumes of *Critical Essays of the
Seventeenth Century* that they are simply essays on Rhetoric.)

(3b) Contrivance or Invention

But Hobbes does not use "contrivance" only in the sense of arrangement; he
also uses it in another sense, namely in the sense of *invention*. This
becomes clear when he praises Homer for his contrivance in which he excels
both Virgil and Lucan. For, says Hobbes, the epics of these two poets are
simply histories in verse, with the only addition of gods who do not appear

in histories. But Homer's epics contain not only many histories, they are
real *cyclopedias*, containing all the learning of his time. They have
therefore furnished the subjects and arguments for all Greek and Latin
tragedies. Here Hobbes again recalls Aristotle's *Poetics*, where he pointed
out that the epic supplies matter for several tragedies.

By *contrivance*, therefore, Hobbes means two different things — *invention*
and *arrangement* — which are the first two parts of classical rhetoric:
invention (*inventio*) dealing with the finding of the material or subject,
and arrangement or disposition (*dispositio*) dealing with the disposition or
structure of the material.

That Hobbes does *not* mean by *contrivance* or invention the same as imagination, especially creative imagination, is apparent from his description of
Homer's epics as real encyclopedias, i.e. as containing all the learning of
his time. For Homer clearly did not invent all this, he simply included in
his poems all the extant, shared, public knowledge of his time. He took
over what was there, he delved into the available knowledge, learning,
subjects, topics. Aristotle's list of *Topics* in his *Rhetoric*, and the later
books of topics and commonplaces in the Middle Ages were simply general
ideas applicable to a great many different subjects of lasting and common
interest, which could serve as themes for orators and poets alike.

Perhaps the prevalent misunderstanding of Hobbes's criticism is due to a
misreading of some of his key terms such as imagination (fancy) and
invention, and their interpretation according to a later, psychological
meaning. The meaning of the term "Invention" has undergone a number of
changes, just like other critical terms, e.g. reason, fancy, imagination,
imitation. By the beginning of the nineteenth century, when imagination
became the hallmark of genius and of the true poet, the older meaning of
invention as the discovery and arrangement of topics and words has almost
disappeared from critical discourse.

(4) Elevation of Fancy

The fourth quality, elevation of fancy, is truly the greatest virtue of
heroic poetry, but only when controlled by discretion or judgement. Men,
Hobbes notes regretfully, admire fancy more than any other faculty, more
than judgement, reason or memory. Therefore fancy is called *wit*, whereas
reason and judgement are regarded as dull and hence unfit for poetry.

It is said that fancy (or poetical fury) makes a poet sublime: and truly,
fancy is the source of both the matter (subject) and words of the poem. But
if the poet lacks discretion (judgement), he cannot distinguish between what
is and what is not proper, "decent" or "fit" for the heroes, times and
places of his epic. Words and metaphors, if used well, are the true
ornaments of the heroic poem.

Here again, Hobbes insists that the difference between a good and a bad poet
is one of language. Words and metaphors must be proper, not too "sharp and
extraordinary", which, though admitted in forensic rhetoric, is inadmissible
in deliberative rhetoric and poetry (p. 70).

Judging the classical poets in the light of this quality, we admire Lucan for
his fancy, but not his heroes. Hobbes repeats the point made earlier that,
whereas in a rhetorician wit alone may be enough, in a poet wit must be
controlled by judgement. Thus Lucan, who exalts only men and not the gods,

shows lack of judgement. But Homer, while presenting some Gods as favouring the Greeks and others the Trojans, makes Jupiter himself impartial. He never prefers the judgement of a man to that of Jupiter or of all the gods together.

Hobbes's main point in this passage is the need of controlling fancy, wit or imagination by judgement, especially moral judgement of right and wrong. The key term here is proper or "fit": the poet must know what actions, feelings, thoughts and words are *proper* for his epic heroes, just as he must know what is proper for men and gods. As we have seen earlier, Hobbes regarded discretion or judgement as the first quality of the poet; he believed that fancy — especially extravagant fancy — had to be kept firmly in check by reason or judgement. As he puts it in the *Leviathan*, "Fancy, without the help of Judgment, is not commended as a Vertue: but the later which is Judgment, and Discretion, is commended for it self, without the help of Fancy." And, although fancy is an intellectual virtue, the source of similitudes and metaphors, he goes on to warn us that "without Steddinesse, and Direction to some End, a great Fancy is one kind of Madnesse ...".[10]

Let me remark in passing that this linking of imagination with madness was to become a commonplace of seventeenth- and eighteenth-century criticism: we find it in Locke, Dryden and Johnson. Again and again they warn their readers against indulging too freely in the pleasures of a wild, uncontrolled imagination. Already in the *Answer to Davenant*, Hobbes decries the use of an extravagant fancy, when noting that "There are some that are not pleased with fiction, unless it be bold, not onely to exceed the *work*, but also the *possibility* of nature; they would have impenetrable Armors, Inchanted Castles, invulnerable bodies, Iron Men, flying Horses, and a thousand other such things, which are easily feigned by them that dare" (p. 61). And in the *Preface to Homer* he again repeats the view that elevation of fancy is overestimated as a virtue of poetry.

(5) Justice and Impartiality of the Poet

The fifth quality is the justice and impartiality of the poet; it applies equally to the historian, for both are dealing with matters of fact. They both must tell the truth about the historical figures they describe. In his history, Tacitus unjustly condemned Roman emperors who couldn't defend their good name, just as the Stoics defamed Epicurus for his evil life. If the poet deals with historical figures, he must be just and impartial.

This virtue is evident in Homer and Virgil, but lacking in Lucan. In his censure of Caesar and praise of Pompey, he shows himself, as Quintilian says, a rhetorician rather than a poet. The other poets, and especially Homer, do not censure their heroes and preserve their good name.

In this passage Hobbes insists on historical truth as an aesthetic criterion. In the *Answer to Davenant* he declared that "as truth is the bound of the Historical, so the Resemblance of truth is the utmost limit of Poetical Liberty"(p. 62). Here, however, he demands not mere resemblance to truth, but historical truth itself.

(6) Imagery

The sixth quality is the perfection of images, comparisons or descriptions,

which ancient writers of rhetoric called *icones*. Virgil compares the fall
of Troy to the felling of a great tree, an apt and beautiful image. A poet
is like a painter, the one painting actions with the best words, the other
painting men and objects with the best colours.

The comparison between poet and painter was a commonplace of Renaissance
criticism. We find it already in Sidney, and it was repeated throughout
the seventeenth and eighteenth centuries. Taken from Horace's *Ut pictura
poesis*, it expressed the period's preference for realistic representation
whether in literature or in painting.

In the clearness of his images or descriptions Homer again excels the other
poets. Virgil took most of his images from Homer, and even if he does have
some images not found in Homer and better than his, this doesn't make him a
better poet. Hobbes compares a passage from the *Iliad*, Book IV, with one
from the *Aeneid*, Book II. Having analysed each passage separately, and
found that their two tree images — the poplar and the old oak — are proper
to their different contexts and the intentions of the poets, Hobbes concludes that neither the descriptions nor the comparisons can be compared.
Homer's image of a fallen man lying on the ground is one thing, Virgil's
image of a fallen kingdom is another. Thus Virgil's images cannot be
regarded as better than Homer's.

Hobbes devotes two whole pages of his essay to a detailed analysis of epic
imagery of two famous passages from the *Iliad* and the *Aeneid*. (It is worth
remarking that in a short modern booklet on *The Epic*, the author chooses
exactly the same passages as examples of successful epic similes.[11])
Hobbes's analysis is one of the earliest examples of such a kind of verbal
analysis of poetic imagery in English criticism. Moreover, we should note
that Hobbes never goes beyond the analysis of the poet's language to that
of the poet's mind.

(7) Variety of Subject

The seventh and last quality of the epic is the amplitude or variety of the
subject. Without it a poem is just like an epigram or one good verse, or a
painting of a hundred figures is just like that of a single figure if drawn
with equal art. In amplitude of matter and multitude of descriptions and
comparisons like shipwrecks, battles, single combats, beauty, passions,
sacrifices, entertainments, Homer has twenty times more than Virgil in his
epics.

Already in the *Answer to Davenant*, Hobbes had noted certain subjects (i.e.
Topics) as being proper for an epic: "Such in *Virgil* are the Funeral games
of *Anchises*, The duel of *Aeneas* and *Turnus*, etc.; and such in yours [i.e.
in *Gondibert*] are *The Hunting, The Bataile, The City Mourning, The Funeral,
The House of Astragon, The Library, and The Temple*, equal to his, or those
of *Homer* whom he imitated" (p. 62).

Hobbes concludes his essay with a piece of advice for the critics, namely
that when they compare the three greatest ancient poets — Homer, Virgil and
Lucan — they should do it in the light of these seven qualities of the
heroic poem. Finally, having shown that Homer excels the other two poets
on all seven counts, Hobbes agrees with ancient and modern critics that
Homer is the greatest of ancient poets.

CONCLUSION

The view I have been arguing for is that Hobbes's critical essays in general, and his *Preface to Homer* in particular, belong to that old and traditional body of studies called Classical Rhetoric. In his frequent use of such terms as "choice of words", word order, "contrivance", "argument", "ancient writers of Eloquence", "Icones", "publique consultation" (i.e. deliberative rhetoric), "Accusation or Defence at the Bar" (i.e. forensic rhetoric), and "Rhetorician"; in his particular reference to Quintilian, who is one of the greatest theorists of ancient rhetoric; in his insistence on the justness and impartiality of the poet (which recalls Aristotle's and Quintilian's insistence on the good moral character of the orator); in all these points Hobbes is in harmony with the main body of traditional rhetoric.

Furthermore, in showing that the difference between good and lesser poets springs from the different language they use, that therefore the epic poet should start with the choice of the best words, proceeding through the best word order to the best arrangement of his subject matter which must be ample and varied; his demand that the poet give to his men what is man's and to the gods what is the gods', Hobbes is in harmony with his time.

Although modern commentators have called Hobbes the father of psychological criticism, I have shown that the *Preface to Homer* and the earlier *Answer to Davenant* are in fact analyses of the language of poetry rather than of the mental phenomenon involved in poetic creation. I have shown that Hobbes was not concerned with rhetoric in the abstract, but in practice. Here too he is in the rhetorical tradition going right back to Aristotle who stressed the practical value of rhetoric as the art or science of speech.

We have seen that in his examination of the seven virtues or qualities of the heroic poem, Hobbes was trying to answer such practical questions as: What are the best words for an epic poem? How should they be arranged? How should the epic plot be constructed? In one word, What are the poet's best means of controlling and influencing his readers?

It is because of the kind of questions he asked, the terms he used and the method he adopted in answering them, i.e. by verbal analysis and comparison between different poets' language, that I have called Hobbes a forerunner of modern criticism.

In such a major twentieth-century work of criticism as Wayne C. Booth's *The Rhetoric of Fiction*, the author tells us in the Preface that his subject "is the technique of non-didactic fiction, viewed as the art of communicating with readers — the rhetorical resources available to the writer of epic, novel, or short story as he tries, consciously or unconsciously, to impose his fictional world upon his reader".[12]

It is because the twentieth century has witnessed a renewed and growing interest in rhetoric as the study of speech and communication, and in the linguistic resources available to writers, dramatists and poets, that Hobbes's criticism is important to us.[13] But its importance lies not, as many believe, in being an early example of psychological criticism deriving from Hobbes's "theory of association of ideas" or "trains of thought"; on the contrary, its importance and relevance for us lies in being the kind of rhetorical, linguistic criticism which has become the most influential and widespread method of our time.

REFERENCES

1. C. D. Thorpe, *The Aesthetic Theory of Thomas Hobbes: With Reference to His Contribution to the Psychological Approach in English Literary Criticism* (New York: Russell & Russell Inc., 1964); G. W. Chapman, ed., *Literary Criticism in England, 1660-1800* (New York: Alfred A. Knopf, 1966), pp. 3-15, esp. p. 12; R. L. Brett, *Fancy and Imagination, The Critical Idiom 6* (London: Methuen & Co. Ltd., 1969), pp. 10-15, 20-23; Martin Kallich, *The Association of Ideas and Critical Theory in Eighteenth-Century England: A History of a Psychological Method in English Criticism* (The Hague, Paris: Mouton, 1970).

2. *Critical Essays of the Seventeenth Century*, Vol. II, 1650-1685, ed. by J. E. Spingarn (Bloomington, London: Indiana Univ. Press, 1968), pp. 54-67.

3. Ibid., pp. 67-76. All references to these two essays by Hobbes are to Spingarn, and I will give page numbers parenthetically in the body of text.

4. Thomas Hobbes, *Leviathan*, edited with an Introduction by C. B. Macpherson (England: Pelican Books, 1968), p. 149.

5. Thomas Hobbes, *Body, Man, and Citizen*, edited with an Introduction by Richard S. Peters (New York, N.Y.: Collier Books, 1962), p. 243.

6. Ibid., p. 190.

7. Ibid., p. 16 and all Part I, "Logic and Methodology", pp. 23-90.

8. John Dryden, "Preface to the *Fables*", in *Essays of John Dryden*, ed. by W. P. Ker (Oxford: Clarendon Press, 1926) Vol. II, p. 252.

9. *A Briefe of the Art of Rhetorique. Containing in Substance all that Aristotle hath written in his Three Bookes of that Subject Except onely what is not applicable to the English Tongue* (London, 1637 ?). In 1651 it was reprinted with other items and in 1681 it was reprinted a third time with a section on rhetoric by Dudley Fenner. See W. S. Howell, *Logic and Rhetoric in England, 1500-1700* (New York: Russell & Russell Inc., 1961), p. 384, for a detailed account of the various reprintings of Hobbes's *Briefe*.

10. *Leviathan*, pp. 135-136.

11. See Paul Merchant, *The Epic, The Critical Idiom 17* (London: Methuen & Co. Ltd., 1971), p. 25, for a comparison between Virgil's simile of Troy's fall in *Aeneid* 2, and Homer's simile of Simoisius' death in *Iliad* 4.

12. Wayne C. Booth, *The Rhetoric of Fiction* (Chicago, London: Univ. of Chicago Press, 1961, 1970), p. 3.

13. In addition to Wayne C. Booth, see, for example, I. A. Richards, *The Philosophy of Rhetoric* (New York and London, 1936); T. S. Eliot, "'Rhetoric' and Poetic Drama" (1919), in *Selected Essays*, 3rd ed. (London: Faber & Faber Ltd., 1951), pp. 37-42; W. K. Wimsatt, *The Verbal Icon* (Kentucky, 1954; London, 1970), especially the Introduction and the essays on style; David Lodge, *Language of Fiction* (London: Routledge & Kegan Paul, 1966, 1970); and Peter Dixon, *Rhetoric, The Critical Idiom 19* (London: Methuen & Co. Ltd., 1971), which includes a good selected bibliography of theoretical and practical rhetorical analyses.

CHAPTER 2

The Rhetorical Approach in Dryden

I

In his book *The Association of Ideas and Critical Theory in Eighteenth-Century England*, Martin Kallich notes regretfully that "In the criticism at the turn of the seventeenth century few explicit applications of the association of ideas to literary critical problems were made. Although there is no doubt that the beliefs of Hobbes and Locke thoroughly pervaded the intellectual milieu of the time, yet few references to the psychological theory can be found in the criticism of the well known writers."[1]

But this is not the generally accepted view. For most modern commentators of Dryden regard him as a disciple and follower of Hobbes — in his general philosophy, political philosophy, psychology, aesthetics and literary criticism. Thus R. L. Brett writes that "Dryden, who was a disciple of Hobbes in political theory, adopted also his account of poetic composition and gave it wide currency."[2] But it is C. D. Thorpe, in his *The Aesthetic Theory of Thomas Hobbes*, who expresses the accepted view of Dryden's literary criticism most clearly. In chapter VII, "The Psychological Approach in Dryden", he states that "Of the professional poets and critics between Hobbes and Addison none offered more fruitful suggestions toward a psychological approach than did Dryden .... He was, moreover, deeply interested in the creative processes involved in poetic composition, and altogether presents a valuable theory of these processes." And, in fact, Thorpe proceeds to show Dryden's great indebtedness to Hobbes in his theoretical and practical criticism. He concludes his account with the decisive statement that "Dryden is, in certain important aspects of his work, clearly in the Hobbian tradition of the psychological approach to aesthetic problems."[3]

It seems to me that all these interpretations of Dryden's literary criticism are wrong or simply off the point. I contend that Dryden's real importance lies not in his supposed application of Hobbes's psychology and aesthetics to literature, but in his dealing with concrete literary and technical problems in which he himself was involved as a poet and dramatist, as well as with those more general literary problems which preoccupied him and his contemporaries. If this view is correct, we will no longer find it necessary to take Dryden to task for changing his opinions, or trace in detail

31

his indebtedness to Hobbes, Longinus, Aristotle, the French and English neoclassical critics; nor shall we regret — as Kallich, for instance, does —
that Dryden failed to apply the associationist psychology to literary
criticism.

We will simply take Dryden as he is: a poet and a critic, whose criticism
sprang from the workshop of his creative writing. And, as the latter
changed and developed, so did his criticism. In this, Dryden is perhaps the
prototype of the English critic, who is not interested in erecting systems
of criticism and aesthetic theories, but whose critical theories are
grounded in practice and observation. If empiricism is the term that best
describes such an approach to literature, then Dryden is an empiricist; but
if it is taken to mean an exact application of philosophical or psychological empiricism, its terms, definitions and laws, then Dryden is not an
empiricist in this sense.

Dryden's real interest is practical rather than theoretical: he is
interested in the formal aspects of poetry and drama, in poetic diction, the
relative values of rhyme and blank verse, of ancient and modern drama, of
French and English drama, the unities, the justification of tragicomedy and
similar problems. As T. S. Eliot, writing about his own criticism, has told
us, it arose out of the creative work he himself was doing. The same is
true of Dryden: as is well known, most, if not all, of his critical essays
appeared as Prefaces or as Dedicatory Epistles to his own plays. Eliot's
criticism presents a working out of the questions and problems he was
facing while actively engaged in writing poems and plays of a new type. As
a writer of poems, plays, heroic poetry and drama, satires, translations and
adaptations of other poets, Dryden also faced a great number of problems
which he had to solve. Were his solutions right, he wondered? How had the
ancient dramatists and poets, the old English poets, the Classical French
dramatists, or the Elizabethan dramatists solved the same problem? How, he
must have wondered, had Homer, Virgil, Ovid, Horace, Lucretius, Shakespeare
and Chaucer achieved their great success? Should he, living in the
seventeenth century, follow in their footsteps? For, if they had stood the
test of time, one had only to do what they had done so well, and be able,
like them, to stir the passions of men, and, by stirring their passions,
give them pleasure.

"... Delight is the chief, if not the only, end of poesy", says Dryden in
A Defence of an Essay of Dramatic Poesy (1668) (Ker, Vol. I, p. 113).[4]
This, we should notice, is different from his famous predecessor's view,
Sidney's, that the end of poetry is both instruction and delight. Living
as he did in a period when religious and moral preoccupations were no longer
very important, at the time of the Restoration, when worldly success and
acceptance by elegant society was much more important, and when poetry
itself was at a low ebb, we can understand that Dryden's main concern both
as a poet and critic would be: How give delight to his audience? And, as
I have already pointed out, Dryden examines ancient, Elizabethan and modern
models in order to find an answer to this specific question.

How then is poetry to achieve its end, which is to give delight? By
imitation, says Dryden, following and quoting Aristotle as his authority.
In *A Parallel of Poetry and Painting* (1695), he repeats Aristotle's view
that imitation of nature gives pleasure: "The imitation of nature is therefore justly constituted as the general, and indeed the only, rule of
pleasing, both in Poetry and Painting" (Ker, Vol. II, p. 137).

Before considering some of Dryden's more important critical views (I use

"views" rather than principles, standards or criteria, because of Dryden's
frequent change of views, which is in keeping with his general eclecticism,
empiricism and scepticism), we might well ask: Is there any common ground
between his numerous critical writings? Any conceptual, philosophical, or
logical framework and foundation for them, which, when discovered, the whole
critical edifice will appear coherent, unified, intelligible? We have seen
that most modern commentators believe there is, and have tried to prove that
Dryden, just like Davenant and Charleton before him, and Dennis, Cowley and
Harvey after him (as well as a number of minor seventeenth-century critics),
is simply a disciple of Hobbes.

It is my contention that, being neither a philosopher nor a psychologist,
Dryden's frequent use of such mental or psychological terms like "wit",
"imagination", "fancy", and "judgement" is *not* to be read as evidence for
any epistemological or psychological theories; that he uses them simply
because they were currently being used in different writings, and, moreover,
he uses them to refer to different things in different contexts. Kallich
therefore accuses Dryden of vagueness in his description of the poetic
process,[5] and Thorpe says that, like his predecessors Davenant and Charleton,
"he employs his terms with some overlapping of meaning".[6]

I said that Dryden uses such concepts as wit, imagination, fancy, judgement
and memory in order to refer to different things in different contexts. In
addition, I hope to show that these words are not at all used by Dryden to
describe some unknown and occult mental and psychological process going on
in the poet before or during his writing, but simply to describe the
finished product of his writing, i.e. the poem, or drama, or opera, itself.
In one word, that Dryden was not concerned with the psychology of the
creative artist and the creative process, but with poetry as a craft, with
the constitutive elements of that craft, i.e. words and their proper use,
and finally with the end products of that craft, i.e. with concrete
specific poems.

As Gilbert Ryle has put it in his discussion of concepts like "Imagination"
and "Intellect", words like "'judgement', 'deduction', 'abstraction' and the
rest belong properly to the classification of the products of pondering and
are mis-rendered when taken as denoting acts of which pondering consists.
They belong not to the vocabulary of biography but to the vocabulary of
reviews of books, lectures, discussions and reports. They are referees'
nouns, not biographers' nouns." It is therefore important to distinguish
between two senses of such words as thought, imagination, fancy, memory,
judgement and the like. For in one sense "we are talking about work in
which a person is at times and for periods engaged". And in another sense
"we are talking about the results of such work".[7]

In our examination of some of Dryden's critical views, expressed in what
have become *loci classici* of neoclassical criticism, we must keep it in mind
that, even when he *seems to* describe the mental processes of thinking,
inventing, arranging one's ideas, imagining, fancying, remembering, etc.,
whether in literal or metaphorical language, he is really talking of the
results reached, i.e. the poetic work itself.

II

In the "Preface to the *Annus Mirabilis*" (1667), Dryden gives the following
metaphorical description of the imagination: "The composition of all poems
is, or ought to be, of wit; and wit in the poet, or *wit writing* (if you will
give me leave to use a school-distinction), is no other than the faculty of

the imagination in the writer, which, like a nimble spaniel, beats over and ranges over the field of memory, till it springs the quarry it hunted after; or, without metaphor, which searches over all the memory for the species or ideas of those things which it designs to represent" (Ker, Vol. I, p. 14).

Dryden had already used the metaphor of the spaniel for the imagination earlier, in the "Epistle Dedicatory of *The Rival Ladies*" (1664): "For imagination in a poet is a faculty so wild and lawless, that like an high-ranging spaniel, it must have clogs tied to it, lest it outrun the judgment" (Ker, Vol. I, p. 8).

These two passages are interesting for several reasons: first, they show Dryden's familiarity with the terminology of the Schools and of the Scholastics: and, as we shall see in the sequel, many of Dryden's critical terms are, in fact, rhetorical; second, we see that Dryden accepts the old faculty psychology, which regarded reason, the intellect or judgement, imagination, fancy and memory as separate and specific mental faculties; and last, but most important, we see that Dryden uses the same term — imagination — to refer to two different things — the mental faculty of the poet, and the product of this faculty, i.e. the finished literary work.

This is clearly shown in the very next sentence, when he says that *"Wit written* is that which is well defined, the happy result of thought, or product of imagination." We should pay attention to the imperceptible change from the phrase "wit writing" to "wit written". For, whereas the former refers to the faculty of the imagination, the latter refers to the product of the imagination. The widespread use of the same word, "imagination", to describe either the poet's activity when actually composing his poem, or the finished product of that activity, the poem itself; or, as Dryden and other critics do, *both* the activity and its product, has resulted in many verbal ambiguities and difficulties in interpreting the critic's meaning correctly. Only a detailed analysis of the various uses of the word "imagination" and its cognates (to image, to imagine, imaginative, imaginary, etc.) can help us differentiate between the different or related meanings of the term in various contexts.

Dryden then proceeds from the general notion of wit to "the proper wit of a heroic or historical poem" which consists "in the delightful imaging of persons, actions, passions, or things". He explains that by "delightful imaging" he means "some lively and apt description, dressed in such colours of speech, that it sets before your eyes the absent object, as perfectly, and more delightfully than nature" (Ker, Vol. I, p. 14).

Here Dryden is clearly describing not the imaginative activity of the poet when writing, but the poem, the finished product. He uses therefore, the traditional rhetorical terms, viz. "apt description" and "colours of speech". The poet, by the power of his language, made vivid with figures of speech, creates in the *reader's imagination* the picture or image of the object described. Here Dryden passes imperceptibly from a description of the poem to what happens in the reader's imagination when reading it. G. W. Chapman, in a footnote to this passage, points out that Dryden is here using "The rhetorical concept of *enargeia* or pictorial vividness."[8] This should come as no surprise to us, for we recall that Dryden had studied under Doctor Busby at Westminster School and was thoroughly trained in the rhetorical disciplines. In fact, as Peter Dixon observes, "In much of his poetry, and in many of his plays, Dryden and his characters are to be found pleading a case or arguing a case; and his critical principles bear the unmistakable stamp of Roman rhetorical theory."[9]

In his view that the poet's creations surpass the work of nature herself, both in perfection and the delight they give to men, Dryden simply repeats in more prosaic words what Sidney had said about the difference between nature and poetry — "her world is brazen, the poets only deliver a golden". There is a striking similarity between Dryden's and Sidney's description of the heroic poem which they regarded as the best and most accomplished kind of poetry. Sidney, in *An Apology for Poetry*, writes: "For, as the image of each action stirreth and instructeth the mind, so the lofty image of such worthies most inflameth the mind with desire to be worthy, and informs with counsel how to be worthy."[10]

Be it noted that Sidney and Dryden use the same word, "imaging" (not "imagining") and "image", in the same sense of picturing or representing. Moreover, in his discussion of the figures of speech, Sidney also insists on the poet's need to show "forcibleness or *energia* (as the Greeks call it)"[11] in his writing, i.e. that pictorial vividness which will enable the reader to imagine clearly the persons, actions, passions or objects presented in the poem.

Finally, Dryden sums up his account of the proper wit of an heroic poem as follows: "So then the first happiness of the poet's imagination is properly invention, or finding of the thought; the second is fancy, or the variation, deriving, or moulding of that thought, as the judgment represents it proper to the subject. The third is elocution, or the art of clothing and adorning that thought, so found and varied, in apt, significant, and sounding words: the quickness of the imagination is seen in the invention, the fertility in the fancy, and the accuracy in the expression" (Ker, Vol. I, p. 15).

This is an important and famous passage, and so it is worth looking at it carefully in order to understand exactly what Dryden says explicitly, what he implies and what conclusions we can draw from it about his theory of poetic composition.

First, we note that there are five different terms which refer to the different mental faculties — imagination, invention, thought, fancy and judgement; and three terms which refer to language — elocution, words and expression.

My analysis of the passage will start from this second part. Dryden says that the words of the poem, in this case the heroic poem, must be "apt, significant, and sounding". The accuracy, truth or propriety of the poet's thought is seen in "the accuracy of the expression". I suggest that the whole first part of the passage is, in fact, superfluous; that Dryden would have made his meaning clearer had he only said that we judge the value of the poem, and the greatness of the poet, *by the way he uses words*. If the words of his poem are appropriate, meaningful and beautiful, the images these words call up in our mind by their pictorial vividness will be equally vivid and lifelike.

Like every literary critic, Dryden too is interested primarily in the literary work itself. He wants to analyse it, to show its "beauties" or faults, he wants to help his readers see and enjoy the work just as he does. He cannot do it by simply expounding and enlarging on the supposed processes going on in the mind of the poet before or during the act of composition. For how can the poet know what he wants to say before he has said it? If we were to take Dryden's account literally — as most modern commentators do — we would get the following description of poetic creation:

> In such a poem, the *Aeneid* for instance, the imagination finds
> (invents) the general idea of the whole — a Trojan hero, who
> after many vicissitudes founds the new Latin nation — and it may
> proceed from there to the general framework of the piece. The
> fancy varies the original sketch, fills in details, derives
> (invents) characters and incidents, molds its materials into a
> whole. Neither it nor the imagination is giving a copy of
> actual people or events stored in the memory; both are creating
> ideal form, though with materials from the memory.[12]

It is clear from the foregoing that Thorpe seems to accept Dryden's account
of the working of the poetic imagination as true. Moreover, he also accepts
without any misgivings the explicit separation of one activity into two —
one mental, the other linguistic. But there is no reason why Dryden —
(or Thorpe) should stop at this point: he could have continued his analysis
of the poet's imagination by saying, for instance, the following: that the
poet, having invented, moulded, varied and arranged the thought must, in
order to find the words that are apt, significant and sounding, *again* use
invention, fancy and judgement, and so on ad *infinitum*.

Whereas Thorpe simply accepts Dryden's account of the working of the poet's
mind by using the terms of faculty psychology, T. S. Eliot's interpretation
of the same passage is different and more sophisticated. In the chapter on
"The Age of John Dryden", of his book *The Use of Poetry and the Use of
Criticism*, Eliot explains one by one every term used, giving it either its
N.E.D. definition, or his own interpretation of its meaning. Arguing that
"'invention' is the first moment in a process only the *whole* of which
Dryden calls 'imagination'", he believes that "elocution" is not a third
act, but only "the last to be completed". He concludes that Dryden's
criticism is modern and analytical, and warns us that "Even if Dryden's
poetry seems to us of a peculiar, and, as it has seemed to many, a
peculiarly unpoetic type, we need not conclude that his mind operated quite
differently from those of poets at other periods; and we must remember his
catholic and discriminating taste in poetry."[13]

Before proceeding to a short criticism of Eliot's interpretation, it is
worth looking at another little-known passage of Dryden's which also deals
with the act of poetic composition. Thirty years after the "Preface to
Annus Mirabilis" (1667), in *A Parallel of Poetry and Painting* (1695), the
preface to his translation of Du Fresnoy's *De Arte Graphica*, Dryden again
describes the act of poetic composition in very similar terms:

> For the moral (as Bossu observes) is the first business of the
> poet, as being the groundwork of his instruction. This being
> formed, he contrives such a design, or fable, as may be most
> suitable to the moral; after this he begins to think of the
> persons whom he is to employ in carrying on his design; and gives
> them the manners which are most proper to their several
> characters. The thoughts and words are the last parts, which give
> beauty and colouring to the piece (Ker, Vol. II, pp. 127-128).

We have seen that Eliot claims Dryden's analysis of the act of poetic
composition to be correct, although worded in such a way that it may lead
the twentieth-century reader astray. Reminding us that after all Dryden's
mind did not operate quite differently from those of poets of other periods,
Eliot thinks that this clinches the whole argument. On the contrary: it is

just this last statement that gives Eliot himself away. For what it shows
is that Eliot himself confuses two things: the actual working of the poet's
mind (or of the mind of any other man, for that matter) and the *language* in
which he or we describe this working (or rather, this supposed working). We
are *not* arguing about the working of Dryden's (or Shakespeare's or Milton's)
mind; anyway, whatever we may say about it is only a matter of surmise or
inference. What we can argue about is only the *language* in which the poet
or critic describes this working (whether actual or supposed), this act or
these acts of poetic creation.

I shall analyse Dryden's critical language in the following section. Here I
am only concerned with the language of Dryden's commentators. In the case
of Eliot, and the language he uses in his interpretation and justification
of Dryden's analysis of the act of poetic creation and composition, we find
that it is a mixture of critical terms: he uses the terms of Romantic
criticism like "fancy" and "imagination" and the new terms of formalist
criticism when he states that "fancy is partly verbal" (although orthodox
formalists would of course say that fancy is wholly verbal). Moreover,
when Eliot claims that Dryden's "'invention' is surely a finding, a
trouvaille", it sounds strange coming from such an inveterate anti-origi-
nality critic as Eliot. Finally, and most seriously, Eliot's analysis of
Dryden's famous passage does not really throw much light on it, and does not
help us understand it better. Whereas Thorpe interprets Dryden's critical
language in terms of Hobbian psychology, Eliot interprets it in terms of
mental processes.

Eliot's interpretation is, I think, symptomatic of many modern critics who
read into a literary text what is not there. Convinced that Dryden is a
great critic, Eliot wants to show that Dryden was making a good analysis of
the act of poetic creation. Therefore Eliot rewords Dryden's account in
modern terms, expressing his own and the generally accepted view of the act
of poetic creation. A poet himself, Eliot knows that poetic activity is not
made up of separate acts or moments, but is one of continual growth, where
the poet's intellectual, emotional and verbal capacities are all engaged,
all the time and at the same time. However, as Gilbert Ryle has convincingly shown in *The Concept of Mind*, both the older theories which spoke of
Reason, the Intellect or the Understanding as a specific faculty or occult
organ, and the newer theories which speak of the specific intellectual
processes of judging, conceiving, supposing, reasoning and the rest, are
equally wrong.[14]

So far my argument has been mainly negative, i.e. I have argued against a
reading of Dryden's criticism either in terms of the older faculty psychology, as Thorpe and others have done, or in terms of the newer theories which
speak of the specific intellectual processes involved in creating and
composing a poem, as Eliot has done. Let us now try a different, and I
think more fruitful, approach to and reading of Dryden's criticism.

III

I think that Dryden's account of poetic composition does not derive from
Hobbes, nor does it tally with modern views of the creative process: it
derives, as I have already noted, from *the art of rhetoric*. His critical
essays show his familiarity with rhetorical terms, principles and disciplines.
And we find him referring with approval to both Cicero (Tully) and
Quintilian, the ancient writers of rhetoric whose books were used in schools
and universities throughout the Middle Ages, the Renaissance and the
Augustan age. Cicero's book *De Oratore* I expounds the skills and rules of

rhetoric in their logical order, viz. invention (*inventio*), arrangement or disposition (*dispositio*), style (*elocutio*), memory and delivery.[15] Dryden's use of the terms invention, variation or moulding for arrangement, and finally elocution, point to his familiarity with the traditional terms of classical rhetoric, rather than with the new terms of associationist psychology.

Dryden refers to Quintilian in the "Preface to *An Evening's Love or the Mock Astrologer*" (1671) and remarks that "I would have more of that *urbana, venusta, salsa, faceta,* and the rest which Quintilian reckons up as the ornaments of wit; ..." (Ker, Vol. I, p. 139).

What are those "ornaments of wit" which ancient writers had and modern writers lack? They had, as Dryden says, refinement, grace, wit and elegance. He does *not* say that they had a greater invention, fancy, imagination or judgement than modern writers. He only says that they had a better command of language, of those figures of thought and speech, those expressive tropes, figures and metaphors which the great poet knows to use, and the great critic to appraise.

That Dryden's main interest is not in the process of poetic creation but in its end-product, not in the poet but in the *poem*, is clearly shown when he observes that

> ... these little critics do not well consider what is the work of a poet, and what the graces of a poem: the story is the least part of either: I mean the foundation of it, before it is modelled by the art of him who writes it; who forms it with more care, by exposing only the beautiful parts of it to view, than a skilful lapidary sets a jewel. On this foundation of the story, the characters are raised.... When this is done, the forming it into acts and scenes, disposing of actions and passions into their proper places, and beautifying both with descriptions, similitudes, and propriety of language, is the principal employment of the poet; as being the largest field of fancy, which is the principal quality required in him: ..." (Ker, Vol. I, p. 146).

In one word, the good poet is a good craftsman, whose craftsmanship is seen in the way he handles the materials of his craft, i.e. words. It is only when the descriptions, similes, metaphors and tropes of the poet are good that Dryden (and we) can infer that the poet has a good "fancy", or imagination, or judgement. But this is merely an inference or an analogy: for, as we have just seen, Dryden passes from the poem to the poet, from the finished work to the workman. In his own words, "the employment of a poet is like that of a curious gunsmith, or watchmaker: the iron or silver is not his own; but they are the least part of that which gives the value: *the price lies wholly in the workmanship*" (Ker, Vol. I, p. 147, my italics).

"The price lies wholly in the workmanship." I have italicised this sentence because it expresses simply, clearly and directly Dryden's whole approach to literature and criticism. It is not the approach and method of a philosopher or a psychologist but of a poet, interested in the materials and methods of his craft, which is to create by means of words such things as poems, dramas, comedies, satires, epics, etc. The difference between a good poet and a bad poet is the same as the difference between a good craftsman and a bad one: the former knows his craft, the latter does not. As Dryden himself puts it, "And he who works dully on a story, without moving laughter in a comedy, or raising concernment in a serious play, is no

more to be accounted a good poet, than a gunsmith of the Minories is to be
compared with the best workman of the town" (Ibid.).

In his longest and most important critical essay, *An Essay of Dramatic
Poesy* (1668), he declares that "the lively imitation of Nature being in the
definition of a play, those which best fulfil that law ought to be esteemed
superior to others" (Ker, Vol. I, p. 68). Having posited the lively
imitation of human nature as the highest end of epic, tragic and comic
poetry, Dryden's next question naturally is: What are the best means for the
attainment of this end? or, in other words, How do the best poets proceed
in their lively portrayal of human passions and humours and the changes of
fortune to which man's life is subject? Dryden's answer to this question is
very modern in tone and, in fact, foreshadows Eliot's answer to the same
question. The answer of Dryden — and of Eliot — is in terms of language;
or, to be more specific, their answer is in terms of those unique characteristics of poetic language to be found only in the greatest poets. In order
to make my meaning clear I shall give the answer in one word: it is
transparency.

Let us first consider Dryden's answer and then Eliot's. Dryden's answer is
to be found scattered in various essays, but we shall look only at the most
important: In the "Preface to *Annus Mirabilis*" (1667) Dryden also declares
that the proper wit of poetry "is some lively and apt description, dressed
in such colours of speech, that it sets before your eyes the absent object,
as perfectly, and more delightfully than nature" (Ker, Vol. I, p. 14). In
other words, if the heroic or epic poem is good, we will *see* the heroes,
their actions, passions, manners, sufferings, *as if* they were actually
happening before our very eyes. Dryden's qualification that the poet's
imitation must be more perfect than nature itself may be taken as indicating
his belief, which he shared with his contemporaries, that the poet must not
only represent but also idealise nature. But this is not our concern here.
What concerns us is Dryden's description of the linguistic means by which
this imitation of nature — or verisimilitude — is to be achieved. The
language must, as he tells us elsewhere, be proper or adequate to the
thought. If great passions are represented, for example, then the words
expressing them must be simple, natural, immediate, not heavy, elaborate
and laboured. As he puts it in the same Preface, "This is the proper wit of
dialogue or discourse, and consequently of the Drama, where all that is said
is supposed to be the effect of sudden thought; which, though it excludes
not the quickness of wit in repartees, yet admits not a too curious election
of words, too frequent allusions, or use of tropes, or, in fine, anything
that shows remoteness of thought or labour in the writer" (Ker, Vol. I,
p. 15).

This is a very important passage, but nothing would have been lost had
Dryden left out the word "wit" altogether. Then it would have been clear to
all commentators that Dryden is not trying to give a psychological description of wit and the passions — whether Hobbian, neo-Hobbian or what not —
but simply a description of what he considers is the best dramatic dialogue.
It is, as I've already noted, to be simple, natural, effortless. If we try
to work out the implications of his words we could say that Dryden believes
that in the best poetry the poet himself is absent; that we are not conscious
of his direction or manipulation of his fictional heroes — neither of their
actions, nor of their thoughts, feelings, and words. This is exactly what
he means in the "Preface to *Albion and Albanius*" (1685), when he observes
that "Propriety of thought is that fancy which arises *naturally* from the
subject, or which the poet adapts to it. Propriety of words is the clothing

of those thoughts with such expressions as are *naturally proper* to them;
and from both these, if they are judiciously performed, the delight of
poetry results" (Ker, Vol. I, p. 271, my italics).

What is clear from the various passages quoted is that Dryden's main
concern is how to achieve a convincing imitation of human nature and life;
that is, of men's actions, thoughts and feelings and of their ways of
expressing them in language. Dryden asks himself: How does a man feel when
in the grip of a strong overpowering passion? Does he have time to think at
all? Does he have time to choose, weigh, select, his words? Or do they just
rush out of him? And his answer is unequivocal: "No man is at leisure to
make sentences and similes when his soul is in agony", he writes in *The
Grounds of Criticism in Tragedy* (1679) (Ker, Vol. I, p. 223).

The poet then must, when presenting the great passions — love, ambition,
anger, fear or hate — write simply and naturally. And the same holds true
for the poet who does not aim at presenting the great passions, but only
presents the manners, humours, foibles and weaknesses of man. Chaucer, for
instance, is a genius, superior even to Ovid, and although Dryden fears his
countrymen will think him "mad for preferring the Englishman to the Roman",
he knows that he is right and proceeds to show it by describing his own
experience when reading the *Canterbury Tales*: "I see Baucis and Philemon as
perfectly before me as if some ancient painter had drawn them; and all the
Pilgrims in the *Canterbury Tales*, their humours, their features, and the
very dress, as distinctly as if I had supped with them at the Tabard in
Southwark. Yet even there, too, the figures of Chaucer are much more
lively, and set in a better light [than those of Ovid] ..." ("Preface to the
Fables" (1700) (Ker, Vol. II, pp. 255-256).

What Dryden is claiming here is what he has been repeating again and again,
namely that the good poet will make us see, feel and experience directly
what he is describing or presenting; that in order to do so his language
must be simple and natural, it must be proper to the passions of his
"feigned persons", who, in their turn, must be seen to experience the real
passions of men. Moreover, in order to move us, the poet himself must be
invisible: we should be conscious neither of his presence, nor of the medium
of language. The language should be so natural that, like a glass, we can
look through it to the world outside: poetic language must be *transparent*.

I noted earlier the great similarity between Dryden and Eliot in their views
concerning the language of poetry. Just like Dryden, Eliot too has written
many critical essays on the drama and poetry — on the experience and
appreciation of poetry and drama, on poetry and music, poetry and philosophy,
poetic imagery, the function of criticism and on the Elizabethan dramatists.
Again like Dryden, as a poet and dramatist, he was naturally interested in
analysing technical problems that arose from and in his writing.

In his essay "Poetry and Drama" (1950), for instance, Eliot analyses the
problems of poetic drama, and the conditions it must fulfil if it is to
justify itself in our own time. He believes that the use of poetry is
justified in a drama "when the dramatic situation has reached such a point
of intensity that poetry becomes the natural utterance, because then it is
the only language in which the emotions can be expressed at all." He then
briefly analyses the opening scene of *Hamlet* ("as well constructed an
opening scene as that of any play ever written"), in order to illustrate how
good poetry works on the audience.— without their being conscious of it:

What we do not notice, when we witness this scene in the theatre,

is the great variation of style. Nothing is superfluous, and
there is no line of poetry which is not justified by its dramatic
value. The first twenty-two lines are built of the simplest words
in the most homely idiom .... No poet has begun to master dramatic
verse until he can write lines which, like these in *Hamlet*, are
transparent. You are consciously attending, not to the poetry,
but to the meaning of the poetry ... at the moment, what we are
aware of is the frosty night, the officers keeping watch on the
battlements, and the foreboding of an ominous action.

And Eliot concludes that "in the immediate impact of this scene we are
unconscious of the medium of its expression".[16]

Dryden too, as we have seen, wanted a poetic language that is natural,
simple and clear. In this, we know, he was not alone: the influence of the
new scientific prose — clear, naked and simple — that was advocated by
the founders of the Royal Society of which Dryden was a member;[17] the
general demand that preachers refrain from religious "enthusiasm" and high-
flown oratory; the belief that words should correspond as closely as
possible to things (a belief ridiculed by Swift in his description of the
Academy of Lagado in the Third Book of *Gulliver's Travels*);[18] the new
empiricism of Hobbes, Locke and Hume, based on the analysis of facts, direct
observation and the experimental method, all contributed to make the
seventeenth century an age of prose rather than of poetry. Indeed, this
tendency was best exemplified in the poetry of the period, which itself very
often resembled versified prose. And, to take Dryden and Pope as examples,
their forte was satire rather than poetry, whether epic or dramatic.

Nevertheless, it would be wrong to conclude that Dryden himself failed to
recognise the importance of metaphorical language for poetry. As he says in
The Author's Apology for Heroic Poetry and Poetic Licence (1677)), "Imaging
is, in itself, the very height and life of Poetry. It is, as Longinus
describes it, a discourse which, by a kind of enthusiasm, or extraordinary
emotion of the soul, *makes it seem to us that we behold the things which the
poet paints*, so as to be pleased with them, and admire them" (Ker, Vol. I,
p. 186, my italics).

Here Dryden expresses his ideal poetic language which is in Eliot's term
"transparent". The whole essay is, as its title indicates, a defence of
poetic licence, i.e. the right of the poet to imagine fictions or beings
which are not to be found in nature, and to present or image them in his
poetry. Imaging, as Dryden points out, is just as much to be found in
comedy as in tragedy and in other poetic genres. It is the very birthright
of the poet, "derived to us from our great forefathers, even from Homer
down to Ben ..." (Ker, Vol. I, p. 189). The thought or imagination of the
poet consists in fiction, and must be expressed by means of tropes and
figures, i.e. by imagery and metaphorical language. Those who criticise and
ridicule poets for using such language do so because they themselves are
unable to write it. "But an image, which is strongly and beautifully set
before the eyes of the reader, will still be poetry when the merry fit is
over, and last when the other is forgotten" (Ker, Vol. I, p. 188).

Himself a poet, Dryden knew that the poet's most important characteristic is
his ability to express his fictions by means of language. But he also knew
that not only poets had this ability: historians had it too. Dryden does
not quote a modern historian, but takes Longinus' example from Herodotus.
The latter uses hyperboles to describe the Lacedemonians' fight to the death
at the straits of Thermopylae, and he is right to do so, "because the hyper-

bole seems not to have been made for the sake of the description, but rather to have been produced from the occasion" (Ker, Vol. I, p. 185). Figures of speech are justified if they are natural, appropriate and necessary, whatever the context.

Dryden here shows an awareness of the general metaphorical nature of language. He knows that an image, when it is apt, natural, strong and beautiful, is easily remembered, whereas a long and wordy description is just as easily forgotten. We can understand, therefore, why Dryden proceeds to a detailed analysis of the different kinds of figurative language in this essay.

The method he uses is really simple: having stated at the beginning that heroic poetry is the highest kind of poetry, he goes on to examine the kind of figures used by ancient and modern poets. He uses classic precedent as his model and authority because, as he points out, Aristotle had done the same: he too, in his *Poetics*, did not enounce abstract rules, but based himself on the tragedies of Euripides, Sophocles and Aeschylus. It is from them that Aristotle derived the tropes and figures. Here Dryden simply expresses the commonsense view, viz. that rules of art are not *a priori* but are derived from practice, from works of literature. (We shall see that Hume will take the same view in his "Of the Standard of Taste".) Works of art, we would say nowadays, are not created according to certain prescribed rules, but they nevertheless embody rules — of grammar, syntax, meaningfulness and structure. In fact, as Wittgenstein says, not only speech, language and literature, but *all* human activities are rule-governed.

As I have noted earlier, we find in Dryden's essay an analysis of the different figures of speech made in the traditional terms of Rhetoric. Thus, observes Dryden, the art of Rhetoric invented names for all those figures which have delighted man in all ages, and therefore tropes, figures, hyperboles and catachreses can and should be used in poetry. As Dryden puts it, "But I will presume for once to tell them, [i.e. these hypercritics] that the boldest strokes of poetry, when they are managed artfully, are those which most delight the reader." Appealing to classical models for justification, Dryden continues that "Virgil and Horace, the severest writers of the severest age, have made frequent use of the hardest metaphors, and of the strongest hyperboles; and in this case the best authority is the best argument; for generally to have pleased, and through all ages, must bear the force of universal tradition" (Ker, Vol. I, p. 183).

We are not surprised that Dryden appeals to the best authority and to those works that have stood the test of time and have universal appeal. This is the standard used throughout the seventeenth and eighteenth centuries, and we shall find it being used by Hume and Johnson. Dryden does *not* say: Virgil and Horace please me, therefore they are good. This kind of judgement, based on one's own feelings, will become the standard literary judgement only much later, in the Romantic age, when the criticism of Wordsworth, Coleridge, Shelley and Keats will have made it acceptable. Dryden stands here opposed to the later Romantic critics, just as he stands opposed to Sidney, who was not afraid to admit, a hundred years earlier, that his heart was stirred at the old ballad of *Chevy Chase*.

Dryden then, as we noted, allows the use of hyperboles and catachreses in poetry. But they are, he adds, "to be used judiciously, and placed in poetry, as heightenings and shadows are in painting, to make the figure bolder, and cause it to stand off to sight" (Ker, Vol. I, p. 184). Following Horace, Dryden often compares poetry to painting, not only in

their common end — imitation of nature — but also in their similar means
for attaining this end. As he puts it in *A Parallel of Poetry and Painting*,
"The imitation of nature is therefore justly constituted as the general, and
indeed the only, rule of pleasing, both in Poetry and Painting" (Ker, Vol.
II, p. 137).

Continuing his analysis of the figures of speech, Dryden shrewdly remarks
that "'Tis true, the boldness of the figures is to be hidden sometimes by
the address of the poet; that they may work their effect upon the mind,
without discovering the art which caused it" (Ker, Vol. I, p. 185). This is
of course true, and is none other than the view expressed in the old dictum
Ars est celare artem. Already in *An Essay of Dramatic Poesy* (1668), Dryden
had declared "that it is the greatest perfection of art to keep itself
undiscovered" (Ker, Vol. I, p. 92). The reader should not be aware of the
poet's art, he should not be aware even of the poetic language, but should
look through the language at the objects and persons presented.

Different writers achieve this ideal in different degrees. No one would
claim, for instance, that in the case of modern writers like James Joyce and
Virginia Woolf we are not aware of their language or of the writer handling
it. We are very much aware of both, because in their case we know and feel
that they are interested in the linguistic medium itself, are exploring
some of its unlimited possibilities and at the same time extending the
immense resources of language. As Eliot has said, "The task of the poet, in
making people comprehend the incomprehensible, demands immense resources of
language; and in developing the language, enriching the meaning of words and
showing how much words can do, he is making possible a much greater range of
emotion and perception for other men, because he gives them the speech in
which more can be expressed."[19] In the case of writers like Lawrence and
Graham Greene, on the other hand, interested in the presentation of
characters and events, in conflict and dramatic situations, the language is
transparent: we are looking through the language at the world, the people,
the places presented. Perhaps this is one of the reasons for calling the
former writers difficult, the latter (comparatively) easy.

To return to Dryden. He was not only convinced of the great importance of
metaphorical language, he was also trying to show when and why it is
justified. Figures, he tells us, "are principally to be used in passion;
when we speak more warmly and with more precipitation than at other times:
for then ... the poet must put on the passion he endeavours to represent:
a man in such an occasion is not cool enough, either to reason rightly, or
to talk calmly. Aggravations are then in their proper places; interrogations, exclamations, hyperbata, or a disordered connection of discourse,
are graceful there, *because they are natural*" (Ker, Vol. I, pp. 185-186, my
italics).

Imagery, figures of speech of whatever sort, are all justified by one over-
riding end — the truth to life or verisimilitude, which is for Dryden the
highest function of literature. The poet must, Dryden maintains, put
himself in the situation of his characters. He must imagine what they
experience, think and feel, and then he will know how they would express
themselves. How does a man in a passion feel, think, speak and act? Does
he reason rightly? Does he talk calmly? No, he does not. He can neither
reason in a logical, connected way, nor can he talk reasonably and
logically. His mind, his feelings, his words, will all be disconnected,
disordered. Therefore, argues Dryden, the poet's language too will have to
be like that: full of questions, exclamations, inversion of the normal order

of words, words improperly used and, finally, exaggerations.

To sum up: Dryden's essay *The Author's Apology for Heroic Poetry and Poetic Licence* is a brilliant exercise in the art of rhetoric. Most of the terms used in his analysis of heroic poetry and justification of poetic licence are the traditional terms of rhetoric — metaphor, hyperbole, tropes, figures, catachreses, interrogations, exclamations, hyperbata. His highly formal or rather technical analysis of poetry makes Dryden not only a neo-classical critic but also a modern one. His criticism is not affective or psychological, but rhetorical, verbal, linguistic. It is, therefore, objective and scientific (for rhetoric is an art or science of speech), rather than subjective and impressionistic. What he has convincingly shown in his essay — as in all his critical essays — is that the best poets are those who are masters of language, who know how to manage it in Dryden's own words with "the coolness and discretion which is necessary to a poet" (Ker, Vol. I, p. 186). Their figures of thought and speech are never merely decorative, but are strong, expressive and moving. As Quintilian in his *Institutio Oratoria* has said, "There is no more effective method of exciting the emotions, than an apt use of figures" (IX. i. 21).[20] This is exactly what Dryden has tried to prove in many of his critical essays, but in the essay we have just considered in particular.

I have examined some of Dryden's views of the nature and function of poetry and some of his pronouncements on the language of poetry, particularly on metaphorical language. I have argued that Dryden is not really interested in the psychological analysis of the working of the poet's imagination (or fancy, or wit, as he sometimes calls it), but is interested in poetry as a craft. And I have shown that in his meticulous (though scattered) utterances on poetic techniques and forms, especially those regarding the figures of speech and thought, Dryden is very modern in his views and method. Time and again Dryden repeats his belief, nay his conviction, that the great poets are great because of their mastery of language. Virgil, Horace, Homer Ovid, Chaucer and Shakespeare are great poets because their language delights us, a delight shared by all people in different ages and countries. All these poets, both ancient and modern, excel in that imaging which is, according to Dryden, "the very height and life of Poetry". The great poet, therefore, "sets before your eyes the absent objects as perfectly and more delightfully than nature". This is for Dryden the ultimate test and the greatest value of literature.

Aristotle had defined poetry and all art as an "imitation of nature". But for Aristotle, just as for the neoclassicists, "nature" did not mean physical, external nature (i.e. mountains, the sea, clouds, woods and flowers) as it came to mean for the Romantics, but only or mainly "human nature". And so it did for Dryden. When, therefore, he tells us in *A Parallel of Poetry and Painting* (1695) that "To imitate Nature well in whatsoever subject, is the perfection of both arts; and that picture, and that poem which comes nearest to the resemblance of Nature, is the best" (Ker, Vol. II, p. 136), he is simply stating the accepted neoclassical view of art as imitation.

Nevertheless, just as for Aristotle, for Dryden too, this imitation of nature is no mere copying, it is something more: it is the imitation not of the given or actual, but of the general, the representative, the universal. We could say that for Dryden, just as for all the neoclassical critics, especially Johnson, the imitation or imaging of human nature as it is would not enable poetry to fulfil its moral function — the presentation of a human nature that is rational, noble and ideal. It comes as no surprise, therefore, to find that, after stating his ideal of imitation of nature,

Dryden goes on to enlarge and explain his meaning:

> As truth is the end of all our speculations, so the discovery of
> it is the pleasure of them; and since a true knowledge of Nature
> gives us pleasure, a lively imitation of it, either in Poetry or
> Painting, must of necessity produce a much greater: for both these
> arts, as I said before, are not only true imitations of Nature,
> but of the best Nature, of that which is wrought up to a nobler
> pitch. They present us with images more perfect than the life in
> any individual; and we have the pleasure to see all the scattered
> beauties of Nature united by a happy chemistry, without its
> deformities or faults. They are imitations of the passions,
> which always move, and therefore consequently please; for without
> motion there can be no delight, which cannot be considered but as
> an active passion. When we view these elevated ideas of nature,
> the result of that view is admiration, which is always the cause
> of pleasure (Ker, Vol. II, pp. 137-138).

In his Introduction to the Essays, W. P. Ker describes this essay as "one
of the less lively of Dryden's critical works" (Ker, Vol. I, p. lxix) and we
could add that it is also one of the less known and little quoted of all his
essays. And yet it contains at least one passage that deserves to be known,
because it is of crucial importance for aesthetics and theoretical criticism.
After stating that "The imitation of Nature is therefore justly constituted
as the general, and indeed the only, rule of pleasing, both in Poetry and
Painting", Dryden remarks:

> But it follows not, that what pleases most in either kind is
> therefore good, but what ought to please. Our depraved appetites,
> and ignorance of the arts, mislead our judgments, and cause us
> often to take that for true imitation of Nature which has no
> resemblance of Nature in it. To inform our judgments, and to
> reform our tastes, rules were invented, that by them we might
> discern when Nature was imitated, and how nearly. I have been
> forced to recapitulate these things, because mankind is not more
> liable to deceit, than it is willing to continue in a pleasing
> error, strengthened by a long habitude (Ker, Vol. II, pp. 136-137).

Dryden concludes that, "Having thus shewn that imitation pleases, and why it
pleases in both these arts, it follows, that some rules of imitation are
necessary to obtain the end; for without rules there can be no art, any more
than there can be a house without a door to conduct you into it" (Ker, Vol.
II, p. 138).

We find here for the first time in English criticism the statement that
there is a fundamental difference between "what pleases" and "what ought to
please", or, in modern terms, the difference between the "is" and the
"ought", a difference as important for aesthetics as it is for ethics. But
it is not the ethical "is-ought" problem that we are concerned with — only
the critical "is-ought" problem. Dryden, the first English critic, puts
here the problem (that was to preoccupy all later critics right up to our
own time) in a nutshell: There are works of art, he says, that we like. But
ought we to like them? This is the central and crucial question. Are they
worthy of being liked? Why ought we to like them? Or perhaps, Why ought we
not to like them? Dryden's answer is in terms of our "deprived appetites"
and "ignorance of the arts". Although he does not say so, what is implied
is that those whose appetites (or desires) are uncorrupted, i.e. good and
pure, and who know the arts, will know the difference between the "is" and

the "ought", between "what pleases" and "what ought to please": they will, in fact, only like what they ought to like, the good works of art, i.e. those works which are true imitations of nature, of the best and noblest nature.

We are witnessing here the beginning of this search for aesthetic standards or norms which will preoccupy all later critics and aestheticians. Being at the beginning of criticism as an independent discipline, Dryden formulated and articulated the problem. The question of the relation between people's actual likes and dislikes and aesthetic standards, between what pleases most people and what ought to please — aesthetically or artistically and not morally — is a question which is still being asked and which has as yet been only partially answered. This is the question of the relation between the standard of taste or of beauty and the criteria for its application. We shall see in the following chapter that the philosopher David Hume will be the first to give the problem its logical formulation.

It is clear, at all events, that Dryden, in his statement that it does not follow that what pleases most in poetry and painting "is therefore good, but what ought to please", shows an awareness that a difference exists, though he does not offer a full solution. Yet his solution in terms of rules of art (or, in modern terms, "criteria" of aesthetic judgement) is the right one. It is Dryden's great merit (and, I believe, till now unrecognised merit) to have been the first English critic to have asked this crucial question.

And, in our own time, Eliot will only repeat the same question in almost the same terms. In "Religion and Literature" he writes:

> For literary judgment we need to be acutely aware of two things
> at once: of 'what we like', and of 'what we *ought* to like'. Few
> people are honest enough to know either. The first means knowing
> what we really feel: very few know that. The second involves
> understanding our short-comings; for we do not really know what we
> ought to like unless we also know why we ought to like it, which
> involves knowing why we don't yet like it. It is not enough to
> understand what we ought to be, unless we know what we are; and we
> do not understand what we are, unless we know what we ought to be.
> The two forms of self-consciousness, knowing what we are and what
> we ought to be, must go together.[21]

REFERENCES

1. Martin Kallich, *The Association of Ideas and Critical Theory in Eighteenth-century England* (The Hague, Paris: Mouton, 1970), pp. 36-37.
2. R. L. Brett, *Fancy and Imagination, The Critical Idiom 6* (London: Methuen & Co. Ltd., 1969), p. 13.
3. C. D. Thorpe, *The Aesthetic Theory of Thomas Hobbes* (New York: Russell & Russell Inc., 1964), p. 220.
4. In *Essays of John Dryden* , ed. W. P. Ker (Oxford, 1926), 2 vols. Subsequent page references will appear in the text.
5. Kallich, op. cit., p. 39.
6. Thorpe, op. cit., p. 149.
7. Gilbert Ryle, *The Concept of Mind* (London: Hutchinson & Co. Ltd., 1949; rpt. 1960), pp. 285-286.
8. *Literary Criticism in England, 1660-1800,* edited with an Introduction by G. W. Chapman (New York: Alfred A. Knopf, 1966), p. 169.

9. Peter Dixon, *Rhetoric, Critical Idiom 19* (London: Methuen & Co. Ltd.,
    1971), p. 61.
10. In *English Critical Texts*, ed. D. J. Enright and E. De Chickera (London:
    Oxford Univ. Press, 1962, 1966), p. 44.
11. Ibid., pp. 26-27.
12. Thorpe, op. cit., p. 195.
13. T. S. Eliot, *The Use of Poetry and the Use of Criticism* (1933; London:
    Faber and Faber Ltd., 1964), pp. 57-58.
14. Op. cit., p. 284.
15. Peter Dixon, *Rhetoric*, p. 24.
16. T. S. Eliot, "Poetry and Drama", in *Selected Prose*, ed. John Hayward
    (Penguin Books, 1953; rpt. 1965), pp. 67-68.

In a lecture delivered in 1933 but never published, Eliot commented on an
argument in favour of "stark directness" put forward in one of D. H.
Lawrence's letters. "This", Eliot said,

> speaks to me of that at which I have long aimed, in writing poetry;
> to write poetry which should be essentially poetry, with nothing
> poetic about it, poetry standing naked in its bare bones, or
> poetry so transparent that we should not see the poetry, but that
> which we are meant to see through the poetry, poetry so trans-
> parent that in reading it we are intent on what the poem *points*
> *at*, and not on the poetry, this seems to me the thing to try for.
> To get *beyond poetry*, as Beethoven, in his later works, strove to
> get *beyond music*. We never succeed, perhaps, but Lawrence's words
> mean this to me, that they express to me what I think that the
> forty or fifty original lines that I have written strive towards."

Quoted in F. O. Matthiessen, *The Achievement of T. S. Eliot: An Essay on the*
Nature of Poetry, 3rd ed. (New York: Oxford Univ. Press, 1959), pp. 89-90,
96.

17. Thomas Sprat, *History of the Royal Society* (1667), in *Critical Essays of*
    the Seventeenth Century, ed. J. E. Spingarn (1908; rpt. Bloomington &
    London: Indiana Univ. Press, 1968), Vol. II, pp. 117-118. In Sprat's
    words, the Royal Society,

> ... have therefore been most rigorous in putting in execution, the
> only Remedy, that can be found for this *extravagance*: and that has
> been, a constant Resolution, to reject all the amplifications,
> digressions, and swellings of style: to return back to the
> primitive purity, and shortness, when *men* deliver'd so many *things*,
> almost in an equal number of *words*. They have exacted from all
> their members, a close, naked, natural way of speaking; positive
> expressions; clear senses; a native easiness: bringing all things
> as near the Mathematical plainess, as they can.

18. Jonathan Swift, *Gulliver's Travels*, Book III, ch. 5, Sec.4. It is worth
    quoting the whole passage:

> The other project was a scheme for entirely abolishing all words
> whatsoever, and this was urged as a great advantage in point of
> health as well as brevity .... An expedient was therefore offered,
> that since words are only names for things, it would be more
> convenient for all men to carry about them such things as were
> necessary to express the particular business they are to discourse
> on ... many of the most learned and wise adhere to the new scheme
> of expressing themselves by things.

19. T. S. Eliot, "Dante", in *Selected Prose*, p. 96.
20. Peter Dixon, *Rhetoric*, p. 44.
21. *Selected Prose*, pp. 40-41.

PART 2

The Eighteenth Century:
The Autonomy of Criticism

CHAPTER 3

A Forgotten Classic: Hume's "Of the Standard of Taste"

I

INTRODUCTION: THE SO-CALLED ANTINOMY

There is a puzzling element in Hume's essay "Of the Standard of Taste" (1757).[1] Not only during his lifetime were critics of the opinion that, instead of fixing and ascertaining the standard of taste as they expected, Hume left them in the same uncertainty as he had found them, but also modern commentators hold that Hume took upon himself an impossible task. On the one hand, he agreed with the commonsense view that beauty is in the eyes of the beholder; and on the other, starting from another commonsense view, he believed in the objectivity and truth of the standard of taste.

These two views are stated by Hume at the beginning of the essay:

> Beauty is no quality in things themselves: It exists merely in the mind which contemplates them; and each mind perceives a different beauty. One person may even perceive deformity, where another is sensible of beauty; and every individual ought to acquiece in his own sentiment, without pretending to regulate those of others ... and the proverb has justly determined it to be fruitless to dispute concerning tastes.

But then Hume goes on to state the opposite view:

> Whoever would assert an equality of genius and elegance between Ogilby and Milton, or Bunyan and Addison, would be thought to defend no less an extravagance, than if he had maintained a mole-hill to be as high as Teneriffe, or a pond as extensive as the ocean (pp. 268-269).

That means, concludes Hume, that no one really believes in the natural equality of tastes.

Modern critics — however different their assumptions and arguments may be — are unanimous on two points: first, that Hume's essay on taste is

important, and second, that he did not succeed in reconciling his two
opposite views, viz. the belief in the subjectivity of tastes and in the
objectivity of a standard of taste.

S. G. Brown, for example, in his article "Observations on Hume's Theory of
Taste", takes Hume's failure for granted. He accounts for it by the fact
that Hume lived in an age of transition, i.e. the eighteenth century when
neoclassicism was on the wane and romanticism was gaining ground. Many of
Hume's contemporaries still believed in the supremacy of reason and understanding, but others were already using new critical terms like "feeling"
and "sentiment". Like his famous contemporary Johnson, Hume too wished to
unite reason with feeling, or, in his own words, "strong sense" with
"sentiment". Hume, in short, was both a classic or neoclassic and a
romantic. Brown concludes that the real significance of the essay is in
being an historical document, a true reflection of the antagonisms of the
late eighteenth century.[2]

Whereas Brown uses the accepted terminology of literary criticism like
"classic", "neoclassic", "romantic", Peter Kivy uses the philosophical terms
"antinomy", "paradox", "subjective relativism", "value-judgements", "factual
judgements". In his article "Hume's Standard of Taste: Breaking the Circle",
Kivy contends that Hume attempted in his essay was to find a solution
to the paradox or "antimony" of taste, i.e. the antinomy between individual
taste which is based on sentiment and the existence of objective standards.

According to Kivy, Hume tries to solve the antinomy by "the translation of
value judgments into factual judgments — judgments of sentiment into
judgments of reason". He agrees with those critics who claim that the
Humean attempt to reduce matters of aesthetic sentiment to matters of fact
is doomed from the start, since disputes about what is beautiful cannot be
resolved by rational methods. In one word, Hume does *not* succeed in solving
the antinomy of taste.[3]

The dichotomy fact-value is, in modern philosophy, traced back to Hume.
But more often than not Hume, in using some of our current philosophical
concepts, neither assigns to them the same meaning nor puts them to the same
use. Both the theory and the method have been misinterpreted in Hume's case:
his theory of human nature and his experimental method have been taken to
be respectively a psychologistic picture of the human mind and a straight-
forward inductive method.

We shall try to show that the objectivity of the Standard of Taste consists
in its being a feeling for common tastes. Furthermore, that all critical
judgements presuppose this standard and hence that we must acknowledge it
as a real existence or matter of fact.

II

THE STANDARD AS A FEELING FOR COMMON TASTE

When our feelings are directed to objects of natural beauty such as people
and natural scenery we speak of "delicacy of passion" or of a feeling for
natural beauty. In the case of works of art, Hume speaks of "delicacy of
taste" or a feeling for artistic beauty.

Whereas in the first case our feelings are natural, spontaneous, immediate
and unreasoned, in the second case they depend on a certain disposition
acquired by practice — a rule-governed practice. Hume's purpose in the

Treatise, the *Enquiries* and the *Essays* is to show how the rules of all
human practices are experimentally evolved. For instance, Hume never doubts
that the origin of the Idea of Justice is in society. It is our social
intercourse which leads us, at some stage, and by using the infinite
possibilities of variations in our passions and sentiments, to form or
invent new feelings, e.g. some general standard. In Hume's words, "The
intercourse of sentiments, therefore, in society and conversation, makes us
form some general inalterable standard, by which we may approve or
disapprove of characters and manners" (*Treatise*, p. 603).[4] The moral
standard, that is the Idea of Justice, gradually acquires force by slow
progress, by men's repeated experience of the inconveniences of trans-
gressing it. Men have recourse to artifice, design, invention, in order to
avoid confusion, chaos and unpredictability: "'Twas, therefore, with a view
to this inconvenience, that men have established those principles, and have
agreed to restrain themselves by general rules, which are unchangeable by
spite and favour, and by particular views of private or public interest.
These rules, then, are artificially invented for a certain purpose, and are
contrary to the common principles of human nature, which accommodate themselves to circumstances and have no stated method of operation" (*Treatise*,
pp. 532-533).

It is, therefore, through a gradual accommodation of natural passions to
newly created conditions which gives men confidence in the future regularity
of their conduct and feelings. It is on the expectation of this regularity
that our approbations or condemnations are founded. This new expectation is
not really an idea (the Idea of Justice), nor is it based on a promise: it
is an artificially invented new way of feeling and its novelty consists in
its direction. It is a feeling for a common or general interest and, by
analogy, a feeling for a common or general taste.[5] In classifying the Idea
of Justice and the Standard of Taste as sentiments or feelings Hume achieves
two of the main principles of his philosophy:

(a) He can explain how these standards are capable of influencing or
     causing actions while still adhering to his view that reason is inert.
(b) Further, he can show that, in the last resort, the application of these
     standards implies a new way of looking at objects, and not the
     discovery of some observable qualities of objects.

Thus there is no antinomy between the sense of beauty we feel before the
establishment of the standard and after its establishment: in both cases
beauty is felt rather than judged. In reading a poem, a man of taste and
feeling will be sensibly touched by every part of the poem. His understanding might help him, but only in the sense of guiding him. If pressed
to give his reasons for relishing the poem, his arguments will implicitly or
explicitly invoke a standard of taste, a feeling which he has acquired by
practice. In short, we attribute to him, says Hume, a "delicacy of taste".

But is this delicacy of taste or, as we have called it, this new way of
looking at things divorced from the observable qualities of the objects? Or
are the latter in some way relevant to the former? In order to answer these
questions we must follow Hume's arguments concerning the foundations in
human nature of the rules governing human practices.

III

RULES AND REALITY

Although Hume does not discuss the relation of the rules of composition to

the standard of taste, we can learn something about it from his discussion
of the relation of the rules of justice to the Idea of Justice, Hume
argues that property, which is a rule of justice, does not consist in any
sensible qualities of the object, "for these may continue invariably the
same while the property changes" (*Treatise*, p. 527). Rules must consist,
therefore, in some relation of the object to something else. But it is not
a relation to other inanimate objects. For, again, these external relations
between objects may continue invariably the same while the rule changes.
This relation, not being any observable quality of the object or an external
and corporeal relation between objects, consists therefore in the relation
of the objects to intelligent and rational beings. It is an internal
relation, "that is, some influence, which the external relations of the
object have on the mind and actions" (ibid.). In a word, nothing among the
observable qualities or relations of an object can explain its being the
property of someone. Property, to be understood, must logically presuppose
the previous fixation of a feeling or sentiment for common interest, that is
the human invention of the idea of justice.

Similarly, rules of composition could not be understood solely by the
analysis of observable qualities of the work of art, for these are sometimes
present in a work and yet we do not enjoy it. For observable qualities and
relations in a work of art to be relevant to a rule of composition we must
logically presuppose the previous fixation of a feeling for artistic
beauty: the standard of taste.

It might be the case that there is a kind of pre-established harmony between
our mental make-up and the natural order of things, a harmony which
determines the kind of standards we adopt. But we cannot go further than
this: to assume tentatively such a hypothesis. To assume such a hypothesis
dogmatically would imply that our knowledge of both the external world and
human nature is an *a priori* knowledge and that all our activities are
governed by rules which are nothing but relations of ideas.

But if the rules of composition are neither generalisations about
objective observable qualities or relations, nor generalisations about
particular feelings of particular individuals, and if they are based on a
feeling for a common taste of artistic beauty, how could Hume speak of the
Standard of Taste as existing and being a matter of fact? At least twice in
the essay "Of the Standard of Taste" Hume uses a language which could easily
mislead his modern readers.[6] Speaking of the rules of composition, Hume
writes: "Their foundation is the same with that of all the practical
sciences, experience; nor are they any thing but general observations,
concerning what has been universally found to please in all countries and in
all ages" (*Essays*, p. 269).

Again, after asking where critics endowed with all the qualities good
critics must have are to be found (and how to distinguish them from false
critics), Hume goes on: "But if we consider the matter aright, these are
questions of fact, not of sentiment", and "Where these doubts occur, men can
do no more than in other disputable questions, which are submitted to the
understanding: They must produce the best arguments, that their invention
suggests to them; they must acknowledge a true and decisive standard to exist
somewhere, to wit real existence and matter of fact; ..." (*Essays*, p. 279).

There are, says Hume, two kinds of systems which we call realities or
existences: "The first of these systems is the object of the memory and the
senses; the second of the judgment" (*Treatise*, p. 108). We form our present
and past impressions, perceptions and memories into a kind of perceptual

system which "we are pleased to call a *reality*". But this reality is less important than the second system of reality connected by custom, by the relation of cause and effect or by any experimental reasoning. Such a reality lies beyond the reach of the senses and memory:

> By means of it I paint the universe in my imagination, and fix my attention on any part of it I please. I form an idea of Rome, which I neither see nor remember; but which is connected with such impressions as I remember to have received from the conversation and books of travellers and historians. This idea of *Rome* I place in a certain situation on the idea of an object, which I call the globe. I join to it the conception of a particular government, and religion, and manners. I look backward and consider its first foundations; its several revolutions, successes, and misfortunes. All this, and every thing else, which I believe, are nothing but ideas; tho' by their force and settled order, arising from custom and the relation of cause and effect, they distinguish themselves from other ideas, which are merely the offspring of the imagination" (ibid.).

Though little quoted, this is a very important and interesting passage. It seems that what Hume wants to say is that a socially recognisable way of arguing leads to a system or a reality called history, systematically to be distinguished from a fictitious history which lacks reality. Similarly, if for over two thousand years the arguments confirming the beauty of Homer's epics are still being used, this means that these critical arguments together with other similar ones lead to a system or reality which we call criticism. In a word, real criticism, as distinguished from false or pseudocriticism, must acknowledge the existence of a Standard of Taste. The permanence of some, nay of many, critical arguments, together with the fact that critics try their best to bring the most cogent arguments to justify their preferences, is a sure sign, according to Hume, that critics *do* appeal to a true standard of taste, a real existence and matter of fact.

In order to understand such a bewildering "subjectivist" construction of objective rules, whether in morals or in criticism, we must refer ourselves to the maxim or principle which has guided Hume in all his enquiries. It is to be found, surprisingly enough, in a very rarely quoted essay entitled *Of the Rise and Progress of the Arts and Sciences* (Essay XIV in *Essays*, Vol. I, pp. 174-197). Here Hume enounces the rule that *"What depends upon a few persons, is in a great measure, to be ascribed to chance, or secret and unknown causes: What arises from a great number, may often be accounted for by determinate and known causes"* (p. 175, author's italics).

However, in the case of the arts and sciences which are cultivated only by the few, it would be natural to conclude that it is impossible to give an account of their origin. Poets, in all ages, have advanced the claim of divine inspiration, of a divine fire by which they are animated. But Hume finds nothing supernatural in this, for

> Their fire is not kindled from heaven. It only runs along the earth; is caught from one breast to another; and burns brightest, where the materials are best prepared, and most happily disposed. The question, therefore, concerning the rise and progress of the arts and sciences, is not altogether a question concerning the taste, genius and spirit of a few, but concerning those of a whole people; and may therefore be accounted for, in some measure, by general causes and principles" (p. 177).

Critics might be very few in number, but this does not necessarily mean that their principles are of a demonstrative nature, i.e. that they are arrived at *a priori* and hence have no reference to reality. Alternatively, the fact that good critics are few in number does not mean that their principles are of a fictitious or secret nature, of an arbitrary or divine origin and hence have no reference to reality. The Standard of Taste acknowledged by critics in their arguments has its origin in people, and hence is a real existence or matter of fact. In Hume's words, "Though the persons, who cultivate the sciences with such astonishing success, as to attract the admiration of posterity, be always few, in all nations and all ages; it is impossible but a share of the same spirit and genius must be antecedently diffused throughout the people among whom they arise, in order to produce, form, and cultivate, from their earliest infancy, the taste and judgment of those eminent writers" (pp. 176–177).

CONCLUSION

Hume argues that the Idea of Justice and the Standard of Taste are, in fact, sentiments or feelings which guide our practices: they are rules. Being neither observable qualities nor external relations of objects, they cannot be perceived. Nevertheless, they *colour* our perceptions of objects and human beings. Hume describes them as "internal relations", i.e. "the relations of objects to intelligent and rational beings".

Our moral and critical discourse includes words which carry their own imperative content. As Hume puts it at the beginning of the essay, "Whoever recommends any moral virtues, really does no more than is implied in the terms themselves. That people, who invented the word *charity*, and used it in a good sense, inculcated more clearly and much more efficaciously, the precept, *be charitable*, than any pretended legislator or prophet, who should insert such a *maxim* in his writings" (*Essays*, p. 268). Similarly, whoever recommends any aesthetic qualities does no more than is implied in the terms themselves; for example, "coherence", "complexity", "unity", "order" or "truth to life".

I hope to have elucidated Hume's theory of criticism by showing the absence of any antinomy, paradox or inconsistency in his essay "Of the Standard of Taste". In sum, for us, the importance of Hume's essay is in being a modern and very subtle analysis of the language of criticism in general, and of the word "Standard" in particular. Hume convincingly shows us that to say "This poem is good" (or "bad") or "This picture is good" (or "bad") implies, without stating it, and logically presupposes the existence of a Standard of Taste for poems and works of art.

REFERENCES

1. David Hume, *Essays Moral, Political and Literary*, Vol. I, ed, T. H. Green and T. H. Grose (rpt. of the new ed., London 1882; Scientia Verlag Aalen, 1964), pp. 266–284.
2. S. G. Brown, "Observations on Hume's Theory of Taste", *English Studies*, Vol. XX (1938).
3. Peter Kivy, "Hume's Standard of Taste: Breaking the Circle", *The British Journal of Aesthetics*, Vol. VII (1967).
4. *A Treatise of Human Nature*, ed. L. A. Selby-Bigge (1888; Oxford: Clarendon Press, 1968).
5. I use the expression "a feeling for a common or general taste" by

analogy with Hume's expression "a general sense of common interest", as found in the *Treatise*, Book III, Sec. II, "Of the Origin of Justice and Property". Here Hume describes how the rules of justice and property are established by the artifice of men, i.e. by convention. But this convention is not a promise, "only a general sense of common interest; which sense all the members of the society express to one another, like that of two men rowing in a boat" (p. 490). In the *Enquiries*, Hume expresses the same idea by the phrase "the general interests of the community". He writes: "The more we converse with mankind, and the greater social intercourse we maintain, the more shall we be familiarized to these general preferences and distinctions, without which our conversation and discourse could scarcely be rendered intelligible to each other.... General language, therefore, being formed for general use, must be moulded on some more general views, and must affix the epithets of praise or blame, in conformity to *sentiments, which arise from the general interests of the community.*" And he concludes that "The intercourse of sentiments ... in society and conversation, makes us form some general unalterable standard, by which we may approve or disapprove of characters and manners." [David Hume, *Enquiries Concerning the Human Understanding and Concerning the Principles of Morals*, ed. L. A. Selby-Bigge, 2nd ed. (rpt. from the posthumous ed. of 1777; Oxford: Clarendon Press, 1970), pp. 228-229, my italics.]

In the essay on taste, Hume insists again and again that "the general rules of art are founded only on experience and on the observation of *the common sentiments of human nature*" (*Essays*, p. 270, my italics).

6. See, for example, Ralph Cohen, "David Hume's Experimental Method and the Theory of Taste", *Journal of English Literary History*, Vol. 25 (1958). Cohen finds that Hume's definition of the standard of taste involves implicit or explicit contradictions. A number of recent articles deal with various aspects of Hume's essay. See, for example, David Kallich, "The Associationist Criticism of Francis Hutcheson and David Hume", *Studies in Philosophy*, Vol. 43 (1946); James Noxon, "Hume's Opinion of Critics", *Journal of Aesthetics and Art Criticism*, Vol. 20 (1961); Harold Osborne, "Hume's Standard and the Diversity of Taste", *The British Journal of Aesthetics*, Vol. 7 (1967); Redding S. Sugg, Jr., "Hume's Search for the Key with the Leathern Thong", *J.A.A.C.* (1957/58); Peter Jones, "Another Look at Hume's of Aesthetic and Moral Judgments", *The Philosophical Quarterly* (1970).

CHAPTER 4

Johnson and Hume

I propose to examine in this chapter only one subject of Johnson's vast critical work and dicta, namely his views regarding the *Rules of Art*. We know that in the eighteenth century many critics, aestheticians and men of letters wrote treatises and essays dealing with the rules, since obedience to the rules of writing (both of poetry and drama) was part and parcel of the neoclassical literary creed. But to compare Johnson's views of the nature and function of the rules with those of some other eighteenth-century critic would not be very illuminating: all it might show us would be certain similarities or differences between them. And since Johnson is undoubtedly the greatest literary critic of his time, not much will be gained by comparing him to a lesser man.

I will therefore compare Johnson's views of the nature of the Rules of Art with those of his great contemporary David Hume. But why, one may well ask, compare the views of a literary critic with those of a philosopher? For surely Hume is known almost exclusively as a philosopher, as the most famous exponent of British empiricism and subjectivism. My aim in comparing Johnson and Hume with regard to the Rules of Art is to build a bridge between these two giants of eighteenth-century literature and thought: a bridge that, unfortunately, did not exist during their lives. For Johnson, as Boswell tells us, hated Hume's "pernicious philosophy". Hume's attitude to Johnson was more tolerant. And we find him mentioned several times in Hume's writings, especially in connection with the Ossianic controversy — i.e. a purely literary matter. In fact, Hume seems to have had a much greater interest in literature than Johnson in philosophy. As Hume writes at the beginning of his short autobiography, *My Own Life* in 1776, "almost all my life has been spent in literary pursuits and occupations".[1]

For Hume is perhaps the last great man of letters who could still take the whole of knowledge for his province. His writings are a synthesis of philosophy, history and literature, thus embodying an ideal which arose with the Renaissance and continued until the Age of Enlightenment. Afterwards specialisation set in.

Both Johnson and Hume believed in the supremacy of literature over the minds and feelings of men. As Hume writes in his essay "Of the Standard of Taste" (1757), "Just expressions of passion and nature are sure, after a little time, to gain public applause, which they maintain forever. Aristotle and Plato, and Epicurus, and Descartes, may successively yield to each other: but Terence and Virgil maintain a universal, undisputed empire over the minds of men. The abstract philosophy of Cicero has lost its credit; the vehemence of his oratory is still the object of our admiration" (*Essays*, pp. 279-280).

And we find Johnson, at the same time (1759), writing the same in almost identical words. In *Rasselas*, ch. X, Imlac says that "the province of poetry is to describe Nature and Passion, which are always the same". It follows that "The business of a poet ... is to examine, not the individual, but the species; ...". And finally, "he must disregard the present laws and opinions, and rise to general and transcendental truths, which will always be the same"[2] (Brown, p. 163).

As men of their time, Johnson and Hume agreed that the end of poetry and literature in general is to describe human nature and passions which are unchanging, which remain constant beneath the fluctuations of tastes and fashions. They also agreed that poets, or rather the great poets, express by means of their poetic language those universal truths about man's life and nature which will last as long as man will last. They agreed that the test of literary greatness is *quod semper, quod ubique*. But they were men of their time not only regarding the aim and function of poetry, but also regarding the means for their attainment. If poetry was to attain its aim, it must, they both believed, be confined by certain rules. As Hume observes, "But though poetry can never submit to exact truth, it must be confined by rules of art, discovered to the author by genius and observation" (p. 270). And Johnson too believed that certain rules are necessary, namely those rules which are "adapted to the natural and invariable constitution of things".

As many critics have observed, Johnson is not against rules *per se*: he is only against the rules prescribed by neoclassical authorities and have no justification except blind obedience to precedent. As Johnson makes quite clear, we must distinguish between "that which is established because it is right, from that which is right only because it is established: ..." (Brown, pp. 222-223). He therefore urges every writer "to distinguish nature from custom". From this and other similar statements it follows that Johnson firmly believes in certain rules as being right, because in accordance with nature and reason. It is logical, therefore, for Johnson to urge an author "to pl.ce some confidence in his own skill, and satisfy himself in the knowledge that he has not deviated from the established laws of composition ..." (p. 221).

Furthermore, Johnson does not hesitate to assert that if "the laws of just writing had been observed", it is natural for a work to become immortal. Such expressions as "the established rules of composition", "the laws of just writing", "the rules of writing", "the rules of stile", "dramatic rules", "more necessary rules", "enthusiasm has its rules" and so on, all point to the same thing, namely that Johnson makes a clear distinction between good rules and bad rules: some rules are "fundamental and indispensable", others merely "useful and convenient". As fundamental and indispensable rules Johnson mentions unity of action in the drama and the need for a single hero; on the other hand such rules as the unity of time and place, the separation of genres, the limitation of the number of personages on the stage to three and the division of a play into five acts, all these Johnson regards "as rules formed by accident, or instituted by example, and therefore always liable to dispute and alteration". Moreover, as he puts it so forcefully in the *Rambler 125*, "every genius produces some innovation which, once invented and approved, subverts the rules which the practice of foregoing authors had established" (p. 222).

If people in general and critics in particular still adhere to fixed and rigid rules, it is because their minds are "prepossessed by mechanical criticism". For Johnson mechanical or formal criticism is simply orthodox neoclassical criticism which had become hardened into such pronouncements as that by John Dennis in his *The Grounds of Criticism in Poetry* (1704), e.g. "there is for poetry, no system of known rules but those which are in Aristotle and his interpreters". Johnson clearly despised such a system of rules, as well as the critics who judged according to it. As he remarked to Fanny Burney, there are three kinds of critics: "The first are those who know no rules, but pronounce entirely from their natural taste and feelings; the second are those who know and judge by rules; and the third are those who know but are above the rules. These last are those you should wish to satisfy. Next to them rate the natural judges; but ever despise those opinions that are formed by the rules" (p. 57).

In sum, those who know the difference between the essential and the inessential, the necessary and the accidental, the natural and the artificial, will need no rules but their reason, commonsense and natural taste. For, as Johnson put it in the *Life of Gray*, "I rejoice to concur with the common reader; for by the common sense of readers uncorrupted with literary prejudices, after all the refinements of subtilty and the dogmatism of learning, must be finally decided all claim to poetical honours" (p. 124).

(a) On Tragicomedy

I

It is interesting to compare the views of Johnson and Hume regarding tragi-comedy. Both back their views by an appeal to "the qualities of human nature", Johnson in order to justify "the practice of uniting gay and solemn subjects", and Hume in order to condemn this practice.

As is well known, one of the most sacred of neoclassical rules of the drama was the rigid separation of the genres: tragedy and comedy were not to be mixed. Tragicomedy was condemned, therefore, and those who wrote such mixed plays were totally disapproved by neoclassical critics who judged by rules.

When Johnson writes in defence of tragicomedy, he does not appeal to those rules of the drama established by custom, and backed by authority and precedent. He hopes that tragicomedies "may chance to please even when they are not critically approved".

Writing in the *Rambler 156* (1751), he defends tragicomedy as justified by nature, reason and human experience. He asks, "For what is there in the mingled drama which impartial reason can condemn? The connexion of important with trivial incidents, since it is not only common but perpetual in the world, may surely be allowed upon the stage, which pretends only to be the mirrour of life." Rejecting the current view that the comic elements in tragedy impair its emotional effect as specious reasoning, he appeals to experience and asks: "Is it not certain that the tragick and comick affections have been moved alternately with equal force, and that no plays have oftener filled the eye with tears, and the breast with palpitation, than those which are variegated with interludes of mirth?"

But Johnson seems afraid to follow his defence of tragicomedy (as being true to nature and human life) to its logical conclusion. Adding that he does "not however think it safe to judge of works of genius by the event", he will not vindicate tragicomedy even by the success of Shakespeare. Possibly, says Johnson, "we might have been more interested in the distress of his

61

heroes had we not been so frequently diverted by the jokes of his
buffoons" (pp. 90-91).

Although, as we see, Johnson's defence of tragicomedy is here only partial,
and he is apparently afraid of saying openly that Shakespeare's success in
his plays, all of which are tragicomedies, is sufficient justification for
rejecting the neoclassical rule against them, we find him fifteen years
later, in his *Preface* to Shakespeare (1765), defending both Shakespeare's
practice and the genre as such. Johnson argues that

> "*Shakespeare's* plays are not in the rigorous and critical sense
> either tragedies or comedies, but compositions of a distinct kind;
> exhibiting the real state of sublunary nature, which partakes of
> good and evil, joy and sorrow, mingled with endless variety of
> proportion and innumerable modes of combination; and expressing
> the course of the world." Although "contrary to the rules of
> criticism ... there is always an appeal open from criticism to
> nature. The end of writing is to instruct; the end of poetry is
> to instruct by pleasing. That the mingled drama may convey all
> the instruction of tragedy or comedy cannot be denied, because it
> includes both in its alternations of exhibition and approaches
> nearer than either to the appearance of life."

Rejecting the objection that since such a method interrupts the passions it
lessens the power to move, he appeals to *experience* in order to prove the
contrary. And he concludes his defence of Shakespeare's successful
practice, as based on experience and human nature, by saying "When
Shakespeare's plan is understood, most of the criticisms of *Rhymer* and
Voltaire will vanish away ... [and] the Gravediggers themselves may be
heard with applause" (pp. 485-486).

By referring to the criticisms of Rymer and Voltaire, Johnson is of course
rejecting the orthodox neoclassical attacks on Shakespeare for not obeying
the rules of the separation of genres and the three dramatic unities. For
Johnson, then, the criticisms of Shakespeare made by such critics as Rymer,
Voltaire and Dennis[3] "are the petty cavils of petty minds", who form their
judgements upon narrower principles than did Shakespeare. Following
Shakespeare's practice, Johnson will accept the one all-embracing rational
rule which is "adherence to general nature".

II

HUME

Both in the *Enquiry Concerning Human Understanding* (1748) and in his
earlier *Treatise of Human Nature* (1739), Hume applies his theory of the
association of ideas to problems of literary criticism. He defends the
neoclassical rule against the mixture of genres as being founded on "the
qualities of human nature". In the *Treatise* (Book II, Pt. ii, Sec. 8),
dealing with the Passions "Of Malice and Envy", he argues that "Shou'd an
author compose a treatise, of which one part was serious and profound,
another light and humorous, every one would condemn so strange a mixture,
and wou'd accuse him of the neglect of all rules of art and criticism.
These rules of art are founded on the qualities of human nature; and the
quality of human nature, which requires a consistency in every performance,
is that which renders the mind incapable of passing in a moment from one
passion and disposition to a quite different one."

Hume proceeds to illustrate this general theoretical position with two examples, one from literature, the other from painting: "Yet this makes us not blame Mr. Prior for joining his *Alma* and his *Solomon* in the same volume; tho' that admirable poet has succeeded perfectly well in the gaiety of the one, as well as in the melancholy of the other. Even supposing the reader sho'd peruse these two compositions without any interval, he wou'd feel little or no difficulty in the change of the passions: Why, but because he considers these performances as entirely different, and by this break in the ideas, breaks the progress of the affections, and hinders the one from influencing or contradicting the other?" (*Treatise*, pp. 379-380).

(As Hume refers to two of Prior's works, "Alma or the Progress of the Mind" and "Solomon on the Vanity of the World" (1718), both dealing with the same theme, one in a gay, the other in a serious vein, it is interesting to note Johnson's views of the same works. *Alma* is "imperfect, because it seems never to have had a plan". But *Solomon* is a work "far from deserving to be neglected. He that shall peruse it will be able to mark many passages, to which he may recur for instruction or delight: many from which the poet may learn to write, and the philosopher to reason" (Brown, pp. 450-451). Surely coming from Johnson this is great praise.

Having illustrated his view against the mixing of genres from literature, Hume proceeds to illustrate it from another art — painting. He argues that "An heroic and burlesque design, united in one picture, wou'd be monstrous; tho' we place two pictures of so opposite a character in the same chamber, and even close by each other, without any scruple or difficulty" (p. 380).

To sum up: for Hume the mixture of gay and solemn subjects, the serious with the light, the profound with the humorous, the heroic with the comic, is simply contrary to human nature and therefore contrary to art. Hume repeats the same view in the "Dissertations on the Passions" (1757) (Vol. IV, pp. 160-161) and in the *Enquiries* (1777).

Although he does not say it explicitly, the very fact that all Shakespeare's plays are tragicomedies (what Johnson called "compositions of a distinct kind") and thus contrary to the neoclassical rule against the mixing of genres, apparently leads Hume to accuse Shakespeare of being unable to write or to reason with propriety. Such a piece of practical neoclassical criticism as Hume's treatment of Shakespeare in his *History of England* (1792) simply shows the fundamental difference between aesthetics and literary criticism, between theory and practice.

For Hume is a philosopher, not a literary critic, just as Johnson is a literary critic and not a philosopher: and both the functions of, and the qualifications for, these two disciplines are different. Hume, for instance, is the first philosopher to prove the logical necessity of the Standard of Taste, i.e. that it is only because all men accept the existence of a standard that particular critical judgements are at all possible and can have meaning. (And that in spite of the great diversity of tastes and the diversity of particular judgements about the same work.) Whereas Johnson in his *Preface to Shakespeare* is seen to possess the very qualities which according to Hume are indispensable for a critic — strong sense, delicate sentiment, practice, ability of making comparisons between different works and poets and freedom from prejudice — Hume, as we shall see in his judgement of Shakespeare, did not. He simply seems to be repeating the accepted neoclassical strictures against Shakespeare without any scruples or misgivings. (We are told that the original version was even more condemnatory than the extant one, but that Hume's friends advised him to tone it down.)

And now let us see what Hume thinks of Shakespeare the man, the poet, and
one of the greatest creative geniuses of all time:

> If Shakespeare be considered as a Man, born in a rude age, and
> educated in the lowest manner, without any instruction either
> from the world or from books, he may be regarded as a progidy;
> If represented as a Poet, capable of furnishing a proper
> entertainment to a refined or intelligent audience, we must abate
> much of his eulogy. In his compositions, we regret, that many
> irregularities, and even absurdities, should so frequently
> disfigure the animated and passionate scenes intermixed with them;
> and at the same time, we perhaps admire the more those beauties,
> on account of their being surrounded with such deformities.
> A striking peculiarity of sentiment, adapted to a singular
> character, he frequently hits, as it were by inspiration; but a
> reasonable propriety of thought he cannot for any time uphold.
> Nervous and picturesque expressions, as well as descriptions,
> abound in him; but it is in vain we look either for purity or
> simplicity of diction. His total ignorance of all theatrical art
> and conduct, however material a defect; yet, as it affects the
> spectator rather than the reader, we can more easily excuse, than
> that want of taste which often prevails in his productions, and
> which gives way only by intervals to the irradiations of genius.
> A great and fertile genius he certainly possessed, and one
> enriched equally with a tragic and comic vein; but he ought to be
> cited as a proof, how dangerous it is to rely on these advantages
> alone for attaining an excellence in the finer arts. And there
> may even remain a suspicion, that we over-rate, if possible, the
> greatness of his genius; in the same manner, as bodies often
> appear more gigantic on account of their being disproportioned and
> mishapen (Vol. VI, pp. 191-192).[4]

(b) On the Dramatic Unities

JOHNSON

Before discussing Johnson's famous attack on the unities which he made both in the *Rambler 156* and the *Preface to Shakespeare*, it may be worth while to recall shortly what the Three Unities were.

Formulated by the dramatic critics of the Renaissance, especially the Italians, they were called the Unities of Action, Time and Place, and supposedly derived from Aristotle's *Poetics*. They ruled that a play should not have a subplot or scenes irrelevant to the action, should not cover more than twenty-four hours and should not have more than one locale. But Aristotle only insists on the unity of action, and simply observes that most plays cover less than a day or "one circuit of the sun"; he does not even mention unity of place. In fact, the unities of time and place were introduced by the Italian critic Castelvetro as late as 1570. The neoclassicist scholars argued that the unity of time and place both strengthened the unity of action and added to the verisimilitude of the play. The rules and their justification were blindly accepted as self-evident truth by the majority of neoclassical critics except Dryden. But it is only after Johnson's stringent attack on the unities of time and place that they were finally abandoned.

Johnson gives the following definition of "the unities" in the *Dictionary* (1755), taken from *Dryden's Preface to All for Love*: "Principle of dramatick writing, by which the tenour of the story, and propriety of presentation is preserved. [e.g.] The *unities* of time, place, and action, are exactly observed" (p. 253).

Johnson, we recall, had little liking for the drama of his time. The modern dramatists, blindly following as they did all the neoclassical rules, produced plays which were possibly correct, but were cold and devoid of passion and could therefore not arouse any passion in the audience. A strict adherence to fixed rules, Johnson realised, did not help, and very often hindered, the drama from fulfilling its true function of holding a mirror up to nature. As Johnson said of Shakespeare, "*Shakespeare* is above

all writers, at least above all modern writers, the poet of nature; the
poet that holds up to his readers a faithful mirrour of manners and of
life."

In his paper in the *Rambler 156* (1751), Johnson divides the laws of
criticism into two kinds: those that are laws of nature and those that are
merely conventions. We have already seen that he regarded the rule against
tragicomedy as being merely conventional, not natural and rational. The
same is true of the Unity of Time and Place. After rejecting the rule of
five acts as one of "The accidental prescriptions of authority", Johnson
continues his attack against the unity of time.

The Unity of Time

> With no greater right to our obedience have the criticks confined
> the dramatick action to a certain number of hours. Probability
> requires that the time of the action should approach somewhat
> nearly to that of exhibition, and those plays will always be
> thought most happily conducted which crowd the greatest variety
> into the least space. But since it will frequently happen that
> some delusion must be admitted, I know not where the limits of
> imagination can be fixed. It is rarely observed that minds, not
> prepossessed by mechanical criticism, feel any offence from the
> extension of the intervals between the acts; nor can I conceive
> it absurd or impossible, that he who can multiply three hours
> into twelve or twenty-four, might image with equal ease a
> greater number" (pp. 82-83).

And many years later, in the *Preface* (1765), he will repeat the same view:
"He that can take the stage at one time for the palace of the *Ptolemies*,
may take it in half an hour for the promontory of *Actium*. Delusion, if
delusion be admitted, has no certain limitation....[5] Time is, of all modes
of existence, most obsequious to the imagination; a lapse of years is as
easily conceived as a passage of hours."

Johnson does not enlarge on the unity of place, dismissing it as a rule
which is simply absurd. As he observes, "The objection arising from the
impossibility of passing the first hour at *Alexandria*, and the next at *Rome*,
supposes, that when the play opens, the spectator really imagines himself
at *Alexandria*, and believes that his walk to the theatre has been a voyage
to *Egypt*, and that he lives in the days of *Antony* and *Cleopatra*." And he
wonders "where is the absurdity of allowing that space to represent first
Athens, and then *Sicily*, which was always known to be neither *Sicily* nor
Athens, but a modern theatre?" (p. 84). Johnson's final conclusion is
"that the unities of time and place are not essential to a just drama, that
though they may sometimes conduce to pleasure, they are always to be
sacrificed to the nobler beauties of variety and instruction; and that a
play, written with nice observation of critical rules, is to be contem-
plated as an elaborate curiosity, as the product of superfluous and
ostentatious art, by which is shewn, rather what is possible, than what is
necessary" (pp. 85-86).

The Unity of Action

Nevertheless, Johnson was convinced of the necessity of one rule for the
drama — the unity of action. Writing about it in the *Rambler 156*, he

says: "There are other rules more fixed and obligatory. It is necessary that of every play the chief action should be single; for since a play represents some transaction, through its regular maturation to its final event, two actions equally important must evidently constitute two plays" (p. 83).

He praises Shakespeare in the *Preface* for observing the unities, especially the unity of action, though admitting that in his plays "no intrigue [is] regularly perplexed and regularly unravelled ... for this is seldom the order of real events, and *Shakespeare* is the poet of nature. But his plan has commonly what *Aristotle* requires, a beginning, a middle, and an end; one event is concatenated with another, and the conclusion follows by easy consequence".

A little later he returns again to his praise of Shakespeare for observing the unity of action, as being essential to the drama: "As nothing is essential to the fable, but unity of action, and as the unities of time and place arise evidently from false assumptions, and, by circumscribing the extent of the drama, lessen its variety, I cannot think it much to be lamented, that they were not known by him, or not observed.... Such violations of rules merely positive, become the comprehensive genius of *Shakespeare*" (p. 486).

In sum, the unity of action is the only essential rule for the drama: and it is a rule which is not *a priori*, but derived from practice and the observation of great works of art and great poets. In the *Rambler 158*, Johnson observes that "we owe few of the rules of writing to the acuteness of criticks, who have generally no other merit than that, having read the works of great authors with attention, they have observed the arrangement of their matter, or the graces of their expression, and then expected honour and reverence for precepts which they never could have invented: so that practice has introduced rules, rather than rules have directed practice."[6]

This last sentence expresses the very essence of Johnson's empirical, practical and experimental approach to the problem of rules of writing and other problems of criticism. It is an approach which is the same as Hume's, though in the case of Hume it was called the experimental method and informed all his philosophical works.

It is worth while to compare Johnson's view of the unities with that of one of the most famous exponents of neoclassicism, namely Corneille. As is well known, Corneille published his *Discourses* as prefaces to his own dramas, expounding in them his dramatic theories. (We recall that Dryden did the same.) In "A Discourse on the Three Unities" (1660), Corneille writes: "The unity of action in tragedy consists in a unity of peril, whether the hero succumb to it or escape."

Regarding the unity of time, he says: "The [dramatic] representation lasts two hours, and would be a perfect resemblance if the action portrayed did not demand more to make it seem real. So let us not stop either with twelve or with twenty-four hours; but let us confine the action of the poem to the smallest space of time we can, that the representation may better approach resemblance and perfection...."

And finally, regarding the unity of place, Corneille observes that "I can find no precept regarding it either in Aristotle or Horace. This has brought some to think that the rule was established only in consequence of

the unity of time, and to be persuaded that one might broaden the stage to
include what distance a man might go and return in twenty-four hours....
I should wish ... that what is represented ... be able to happen in a private
room or salon ... but often that is so awkward, not to say impossible, that
some enlargement of place must of necessity be found, as also of time."[7]

What is most striking about this discourse is that, written a hundred years
before Johnson, the great French classical dramatist makes the same
observations about the unity of place, and has the same strictures against a
strict obedience to the rules of the unities of time and place. In fact,
just like Johnson, Corneille also regards the unity of action as the most
important.

II

HUME ON THE UNITY OF ACTION

It is as early as 1734 that Hume, in a letter to a friend, writes of his
resolution to make human nature his principal study, and the source from
which he "would derive every Truth in Criticism, as well as Morality". And
this is, as we know, exactly what he undertook in his many philosophical
writings that were to follow. Although it is only much later, in the *Four
Dissertations* (1757), that we find his essays "Of Tragedy" and "Of the
Standard of Taste" dealing with the philosophical basis of literary
criticism, there are various observations on literature and literary theory
scattered both in the *Treatise* (1739) and the early editions of the *Enquiry*
(1748). (In what follows I shall refer to the latter. The text of the
passages quoted may be found in the footnotes of the *Enquiry*, ed. Green and
Grose, Vol. IV, pp. 19-23.)

We must remember that Hume is not, like Johnson, a literary critic. If and
when he deals with literary problems it is mostly to support or illustrate
his theory about the workings of the mind, namely his theory of the
connexion or association of ideas. We are not surprised, therefore, to find
that Hume does not deal with such specifically literary problems as the
unities of time and place. He does, nevertheless, refer in several
passages to the most important unity — the unity of action.

Writing about this matter, Hume states at the beginning that every writer of
a literary work must, before he even begins to write, have a plan or design,
otherwise his product would resemble the raving of a madman. The writer
therefore, Hume continues, has to connect the various parts of his work so
that they "form a kind of *Unity*, which may bring them under one plan or
view". This unity of action, being a structural principle, applies equally
to all literary genres — biography, history, the epic and drama, and
"admits of no exception". Observing that "Here therefore, we may attain
some notion of that *Unity of Action*, about which all critics, after
Aristotle, have talked so much. Perhaps to little purpose", he adds
ironically, "while they directed not their taste or sentiment by the
accuracy of philosophy" [meaning, of course, his own philosophy]. He then
proceeds to give a psychological grounding to the unity of action:

> 'Tis evident, that in a just composition, all the affections,
> excited by the different events, described and represented, add
> mutual force to each other; and that while the heroes are all
> engaged in one common scene, and each action is strongly connected
> with the whole, the concern is continually awake, and the passions
> make an easy transition from one object to another. The strong

connection of events, as it facilitates the passage of the thought
or imagination from one to another, facilitates also the trans-
fusion of the passions, and preserves the affections still in the
same channel and direction. Our sympathy and concern for Eve
prepares the way for a like sympathy with Adam: The affection is
preserved almost entire in the transition; and the mind seizes
immediately the new object as strongly related to that which
formerly engaged its attention. But were the poet to make a total
digression from his subject, and introduce a new actor, nowise
connected with the personages, the imagination, feeling a breach
in the transition, would enter coldly into the new scene, would
kindle by slow degrees; and in returning to the main subject of
the poem, would pass, as it were, upon foreign ground, and have
its concern to excite anew, in order to take part with the
principal actors (Vol. IV, p. 21n).

Finally, Hume suggests that "By introducing into any composition, personages
and actions, foreign to each other, an injudicious author loses that
communication of emotions by which alone he can interest the heart, and
raise the passions to their proper height and period." Hume concludes that
both Homer and Milton observe that unity of action without which, as he said
earlier, an author "loses that communication of emotions by which alone he
can interest the heart" (Vol. IV, p. 23n).

Whereas in Book I of the *Treatise*, "Of the Understanding", Hume described
the self as a mere bundle or collection of impressions (or perceptions), in
Book II, "Of the Passions", he often speaks in terms of the unity of the
self, either one's own or the self of others. We must remember that the
"indirect passions" — pride, humility, love and hate — have a special
relation to the self, one's own self and the self of others. Whatever
Hume's philosophical doubts about "the idea of the self" or personal
identity may have been, he knew that he couldn't explain the emotional life
of the individual person without some account of the awareness of personal
identity. Thus, for example, though pride and humility may have different
causes, their *object* (according to Hume) is always the same, namely *the
self*.

It may well be that strong *literary* influences were at work in Hume's
different treatment of the self in the two books of the *Treatise*. But it is
Book II, "Of the Passions", that is of special interest for literary theory,
since it is these strong, universal human passions of love, hate and pride
or self-esteem that are the basic themes of tragedy. And the *unity of action*
in the drama presupposes and expresses a unitary conception of human nature.

(c) On Style

I

JOHNSON

Although Johnson is often regarded "as the last great defender of the neoclassical faith", even his most adverse critics will have to admit that, in
spite of his "orthodoxy", he showed his independence, or rather his hetero-
doxy, in many literary matters. For Johnson was ready to challenge
established critical judgements, public opinion and reigning favourites.
His attacks on the poets Gray and Prior, his *Life of Milton* with his
adverse criticism of *Samson Agonistes* and *Lycidas*, are well-known instances
of his fearless independent judgement. As J. E. Brown says in a footnote in
his *The Critical Opinions of Samuel Johnson*:

> "His friends testified to the independence of his criticism, e.g.
> Murphy wrote: 'In matters of criticism, Johnson is never the echo
> of preceding writers. He thinks and decides for himself' (John.
> Misc. 1. 469). And Tyers commented on the *Lives of the Poets*:
> 'He took no poet from the shelf, neither Aristotle, Bossu, nor
> Boileau. He hardly liked to quote, much more to steal. He drew
> his judgments from principles of human nature ... before the
> *Elements of Criticism*, by Lord Kames, made their appearance' (John.
> Misc. 2. 372)."

This independence of judgement is, I believe, most clearly seen in his
various comments on the style of writing in general, and his views of what
is the best style in particular. We find it in the *Preface to Shakespeare*:

> If there be, what I believe there is, in every nation, a stile
> which never becomes obsolete, a certain mode of phraseology so
> consonant and congenial to the analogy and principles of its
> respective language as to remain settled and unaltered; this style
> is probably to be sought in the common intercourse of life, among
> those who speak to be understood, without ambition of elegance.
> The polite are always catching modish innovations, and the learned
> depart from established forms of speech, in hope of finding or

> making better ... but there is a conversation above grossness and
> below refinement, where propriety resides ... (p. 240).

Johnson makes several important points in this passage: first, that there is
a style which will never become obsolete or old-fashioned; second, that the
reason for this is to be found in the nature of the style, i.e. its naturalness. What is natural, that is what is in accordance with the principles of
human nature, is reflected in the principles of the different languages.
Johnson assumes that men, at all events most men, speak in order to be
understood, not in order to hide or obscure their thought by elegant refinements or modish innovations. If communication is the aim both of speech and
writing, then, says Johnson, the best style is the one best adapted to make
communication of thought and feeling easy and understandable. Whatever
hinders communication and understanding is superfluous, is mere ornament.
But literature, Johnson knows, is not the same as "the common intercourse of
life"; it cannot succeed as literature unless it pleases. As Johnson so
confidently asserts in his famous dictum, "The end of writing is to instruct;
the end of poetry is to instruct by pleasing" (p. 3).

One of the best means of pleasing is a good style. There is all the
difference in the world between a writer who is good because he has a
conscious moral purpose and a writer who expresses his moral purpose with
imaginative power, i.e. in a good style. As Imlac says (in ch.X in
Rasselas), the poet who "must write as the interpreter of nature, and the
legislator of mankind" must cultivate a style that is worthy of his thoughts,
with "every delicacy of speech and grace of harmony" (pp. 198-199). Johson
firmly believes that the end of poetry is to express "general and
transcendental truths, which will always be the same", and believes just as
firmly that "the end of poetry is pleasure". If this is so, it follows that
"That book is good in vain which the reader throws away". It needs no
argument to show that one of the main sources of the pleasure given by
works of literature is a good style.

What then is a good style? In trying to answer this question, we recall
Johnson's famous reply when Boswell asked him "What is poetry?" "Why, Sir,
it is much easier to say what it is not. We all *know* what light is; but it
is not easy to *tell* what it is" (p. 199).

In the *Life of Pope*, Johnson again insists that "To circumscribe poetry by a
definition will only show the narrowness of the definer ..." (p. 202). And
because poetry is, of all the literary genres, the one most intractable to
definition, we are not surprised that with his staunch common sense Johnson
did not attempt to define it.

Just as we cannot circumscribe poetry by an exact definition, we cannot
define "good style": it is much easier to point out what we mean by a good
style (or a bad one) by giving examples of good or bad writing. For it is
then that we *see* the different qualities of different styles embodied in
concrete form. Be it added that Johnson, while classifying style into
three forms, "the *familiar*, the *solemn* and the *pathetick*", proceeds exactly
in this practical, empirical way. He never discusses the difference between
a good and a bad style in the abstract. When, for example, he praises
Shakespeare for his good, natural style, he gives numerous examples of it in
his appreciation of individual plays. Similarly, when he wants to explain
what he means by a bad style, he writes in the *Idler 36* (1758): "There is a
mode of style for which I know not that the masters of oratory have yet
found a name, a style by which the most evident truths are so obscured, that
they can no longer be perceived, and the most familiar propositions so

disguised that they cannot be known."

He calls this style the "terrifick", or the "repulsive", or in plain English the "bugbear" style, illustrating it with a passage from *Letters Concerning Mind* by John Petvin, vicar of Islington, Devon, who begins by declaring that "the sorts of things are things that now are, have been, and shall be, and the things that strictly Are". The author continues that "the Ares, in the former sense, are things that lie between the Have-beens and Shall-bes. The Have-beens are things that are past ...",[8] and so on for a whole paragraph, and presumably for the whole book.

As we can see from the foregoing, Johnson believed that plain truths are best expressed in plain language; however, both in prose and in poetry he preferred a style which was neither too simple, nor too ornamental; it should have both simplicity and ornament, but in just proportion. Johnson called it the "familiar" or "easy style" in poetry, the "middle style" in prose. Writing in the *Idler 77*, he says that "Easy poetry is that in which natural thoughts are expressed without violence to the language. The discriminating character of ease consists principally in the diction, for all true poetry requires that the sentiment be natural." Such poetry will be "understood as long as the language lasts". It excludes pomp, but not greatness and wit. Its qualities are "naked elegance and simple purity", requiring great care and skill from the poet. Given these stringent demands, Johnson doubts "whether any of our authors has as yet been able, for twenty lines together, nicely to observe the true definition of easy poetry" (p. 239).

But Johnson has no doubts in the case of the best prose style, "the middle style". Thus, writing in the *Life of Addison*, he declares that "His prose is the model of the middle style; on grave subjects not formal, on light occasions not groveling; pure without scrupulosity, and exact without apparent elaboration; always equable, and always easy, without glowing words or polished sentences." And he concludes that "Whoever wishes to attain an English style, familiar but not coarse, and elegant but not ostentatious, must give his days and nights to the volumes of Addison" (pp. 270-271).

"Familiar but not coarse, and elegant but not ostentatious" — this is Johnson's clear and succinct description of the good style: and it applies equally to prose and to poetry. By contrast, Johnson rejects the coarse and ostentatious, everything that obscures and disguises thought, everything that departs "from established forms of speech", either by the use of modish innovations or abstruse, learned terms. Just as natural sentiments demand a natural expression, false sentiments are often clothed in a pompous, ostentatious, grandiloquent style. As Johnson puts it, "Any epithet which can be ejected without diminution of the sense, any curious iteration of the same word, and all unusual, though not ungrammatical structure of speech, destroy the grace of easy poetry." He censures poets whose lines are "swelled with epithets, brightened by figures, and stiffened by transpositions", because their poetry can be neither good nor serious (p. 239).

Finally, in spite of Johnson's many strictures against Milton as a dramatist and poet, he praises *Samson Agonistes* for its language which "is through the whole dialogue remarkably simple and unadorned, seldom heightened by epithets, or varied by figures ..." (p. 409).

To sum up: for Johnson the best style is one that is familiar yet elegant, clear, simple and unadorned, springing from "the common intercourse of life". It is the style best suited for the expression of those general and transcendental truths which will always be the same. Johnson's views and demands regarding good style recall the demands made a hundred years earlier by the founders of the Royal Society. Thomas Sprat, in his *History of the Royal Society* (1667), reports that the founding members of the Society have made a "Resolution, to reject all the amplifications, digressions, and swellings of style; to return back to the primitive purity, and shortness, when men deliver'd so many *things*, almost in an equal number of *words*. They have exacted from all their members, a close, naked, natural way of speaking; positive expressions; clearness; a native easiness; bringing all things as near the Mathematical plainness, as they can."[9]

Commenting about this book, Johnson calls it "one of the few books which selection of sentiment and elegance of diction have been able to preserve, though written upon a subject flux and transitory" (p. 513). As far as the Society's view of the best style is concerned, Johnson would have given it his wholehearted support. Like the members of the Royal Society, he too was engaged in the same attempt to reform the language, to free both poetry and prose from affectation, obscurity, far-fetched similes, puns, verbal conceits, unusual or learned words, superfluous epithets and empty rhetoric.

In order to achieve this aim he chose "the middle way", in the sense of "nothing in excess". But Johnson is both critic and moralist, both critic of literature and manners. We are not surprised, therefore, to find that "the middle way" is for Johnson not only a rule of style, but also a rule of conduct. It is this rule he affirms and defends in his essay "Mediocrity: A Fable" in the *Rambler 38*. At the beginning of the essay, he writes: "Among many parallels which men of imagination have drawn between the natural and moral state of the world, it has been observed that happiness, as well as virtue, consists in mediocrity; that to avoid every extreme is necessary even to him who has no other care than to pass through the present state with ease and safety; and that the middle path is the road of security, on either side of which are not only the pitfalls of vice but the precipices of ruin."

For Johnson, then, the good life and the good style consist in "the middle way". It is the same view that Aristotle expounded in his *Ethics* and his *Poetics*.

In the *Poetics*, ch. XXII, Aristotle writes:

> The greatest virtue of diction is to be clear without being commonplace. The clearest diction is that which consists of words in everyday use, but this is commonplace, as can be seen in the poetry of Cleophon and Sthenelus. On the other hand, a diction abounding in unfamiliar usages has dignity, and is raised above the everyday level. By unfamiliar usages I mean loan-words, metaphors, expanded forms, and anything else that is out of the ordinary. However, the exclusive use of forms of this kind would result either in a riddle or in barbarism — a riddle if they are metaphorical, barbarism if they were all importations.

In the following paragraph Aristotle explains how such a good diction is achieved: "Among the most effective means of achieving both clarity of diction and a certain dignity is the use of expanded, abbreviated, and altered forms of words; the unfamiliarity due to this deviation from normal usages will raise the diction above the commonplace, while the retention of some parts of the normal forms will make for clarity."[10] Johnson could not have agreed more.

In *The Nicomachean Ethics*, Book II, ch. vi, Aristotle illustrates what he means by goodness and the good man:

> By 'goodness' I mean goodness of moral character, since it is moral goodness that deals with feelings and actions, and it is in them that we find excess, deficiency, and a mean. It is possible, for example, to experience fear, boldness, desire, anger, pity, and pleasures and pains generally, too much or too little or to the right amount. But to have these feelings at the right times on the right occasions towards the right people for the right motive and in the right way is to have them in the right measure, that is, somewhere between the extremes; and this is what characterizes goodness.... Goodness, then, is a mean condition in the sense that it aims at and hits the mean.[11]

It is exactly this ideal of conduct that Johnson expounded and defended in his "Mediocrity: A Fable" in the *Rambler 38*.

II

HUME

It is well known that Hume is one of the great masters of English prose. Johnson, we recall, made only few references to Hume in his writings, and all of them were disparaging, both regarding Hume's thought and his language. While admitting that he had not read Hume's historical writings, Johnson must have read his philosophical works because he refers to "His pernicious philosophy". As to his style, he remarked that "Hume has taken his style from Voltaire." Therefore, he told Boswell, "Why, Sir, his style is not English; the structure of his sentences is French" (p. 376). As Boswell reports, Johnson could never hear Hume mentioned without losing his temper, and he even went so far as to leave the house of a friend when hearing that Hume too was invited. Whatever the reasons for this violent prejudice against Hume, it is remarkable to note the great similarity of their views on many subjects relating to literature and literary criticism. We have already examined their similar views on tragicomedy and the unities. We shall find the same is true with regard to style.

In his essay "Of the Standard of Taste", Hume observes that our use of common critical and moral terms often conceals basic differences of opinion. Thus, although "Every voice is united in applauding elegance, propriety, simplicity, spirit in writing; and in blaming fustian, affectation, coldness, and a false brilliancy: But when critics come to particulars, this seeming unanimity vanishes; and it is found that they had affixed a very different meaning to their expression" (*Essays*, p. 266).

In this short passage Hume gives us in fact what he considers the qualities of a good style and a bad style respectively. Elegance, propriety, simplicity on the one hand, versus fustian, affectation, coldness and a false brilliance on the other. As we have seen, Johnson too regarded them as the qualities of good and bad writing.

In Essay XX, "Of Simplicity and Refinement in Writing", Hume examines different kinds of style in order to find what constitutes good style. He begins with a definition of fine writing taken from Addison: "Fine writing, according to Mr. Addison, consists of sentiments, which are natural, without being obvious", and adds that "There cannot be a juster, and a more concise definition of fine writing" (p. 240).

What strikes one immediately is that both Hume and Johnson cite Addison to support their views of good style. But whereas Hume cites Addison's theoretical definition of "fine writing", Johnson cites him as a living example of good writing, a model worthy of imitation. ("Whoever wishes to attain an English style, familiar but not coarse, and elegant but not ostentatious, must give his days and nights to the volumes of Addison" [Brown, p. 271].)

Since "Sentiments, which are merely natural, affect not the mind with any pleasure", Hume claims that "Nothing can please persons of taste, but nature drawn with all her graces and ornaments, *la belle nature*." It follows that nature and simplicity alone are not enough; something more is needed. If the language of an orator, philosopher, critic or author "be not elegant, his observations uncommon, his sense strong and masculine, he will in vain boast his nature and simplicity."

Yet elegance does not imply excessive refinements. As Hume puts it, "Too much ornament is a fault of every kind of production. Uncommon expressions, strong flashes of wit, pointed similes, and epigrammatic turns, especially when they occur too frequently, are a disfigurement, rather than an embellishment of discourse." An overabundance of wit is just as bad as an overabundance of conceits. Both are to be rejected as different kinds of excess (pp. 240-241).

What then is good style? Hume makes three general observations on that head:

"First ... That though excesses of both kinds are to be avoided, and though a proper medium ought to be studied in all productions; yet this medium lies not in a point, but admits of a considerable latitude." Hume believes that "Of all great poets, Virgil and Racine ... lie nearest the center, and are farthest removed from both extremities" (p. 241).

His second observation is *"That it is very difficult, if not impossible, to explain by words where the just medium lies between the excesses of simplicity and refinement, or to give any rule by which we can know precisely the bounds between the fault and the beauty"* (pp. 240-241).

On this point there is, says Hume, universal agreement, in spite of the great variety of tastes. Beauty as well as virtue lies in a medium. Hume's ideal we notice, is the same as Aristotle's in *The Nicomachean Ethics*, Book II (quoted earlier), and the same as Johnson's "middle way".

Hume's third and last observation on this subject is *"That we ought to be more on our guard against the excess of refinement than that of simplicity; and that because the former excess is both less* beautiful, *and more* dangerous *than the latter"* (p. 242, author's italics).

Hume concludes with a warning against "the excess of refinement which is now more to be guarded against then ever" and sees in France as well as in England "symptoms of a like degeneracy of taste" (pp. 243-244).

It is clear from the foregoing that Hume, just like Johnson and Aristotle, advocated an avoidance of extremes, both in ethics and in literature. The best conduct, just like the best style, is one that embodies the golden mean, the mean in actions and in language. Excess of whatever kind is bad. Excess of elegance, like excess of simplicity, is in bad taste. In fact, bad writing is the verbal expression of bad taste. Good writing, or good style, is one having simple refinement or refined simplicity.

As we have seen, Hume takes the view that rules of writing and of criticism presuppose a Standard of Taste: a standard developed through the practice of creating, writing, reading, analysing, discussing and evaluating works of literature; a standard that is not innate and *a priori*, but invented by man and hence *a posteriori*.

Johnson, we recall, takes the same view: that rules of writing and of criticism are not *a priori* but *a posteriori*, founded on practice and experience, "so that practice has introduced rules, rather than rules have directed practice". We noted his strong opposition to all the edicts of self-proclaimed legislators, i.e. those orthodox neoclassicists who "prohibited new experiments of wit, restrained fancy from the indulgence of her innate inclination to hazard and adventure, and condemned all future flights of genius to pursue the path of the Meonian eagle" [i.e. Homer] (p. 223).

Johnson's use of such terms as "new experiments of wit", the "innate inclination to hazard and adventure" of fancy, the "flights of genius", and "practice" as the ground for the discovery of rules clearly shows that the road was already open for a new kind of criticism — the Romantic. Moreover, Johnson did not share the orthodox neoclassical creed of such critics as Rymer and Dennis in a canon of poetic and dramatic rules derived from the great models of antiquity and belonging to a past age. Seeing that rules of writing and of criticism derive from literary works, and new works are continually being created, he had no doubts that new rules of writing and criticism were also being created at the same time. Whatever we may think of Johnson's general critical principles, pronouncements, definitions and dicta, his views about the rules (of writing and of criticism) are definitely ahead of his time: in this, at all events, he is a modern.

It will come as no surprise for us to find that when Coleridge will discuss the rules in his *Biographia Literaria*, his remarks will seem so familiar: for we have already encountered them before, in Johnson. In fact, the critical theory of the Romantics will not at all seem revolutionary or strange to us — for the simple reason that in history, in literature and in literary history there are no distinct periods called neoclassic and romantic. There are only poets, writers and critics with a certain style of writing, where we can discern certain characteristics, which we then proceed to label as neoclassic or romantic respectively. But, as I noted earlier, in reality such a clear-cut division simply does not exist — it is an invention of critics, literary historians and theorists.

Nevertheless, what we can do is an analysis of the language used by poets and critics in order to discover their key terms from which we infer their principles, views, theories, body of aesthetic and ethical beliefs and finally philosophy. Thus, we are justified in saying that the central concepts of eighteenth-century thought (critical, moral and political) are nature, reason and truth, the central concepts of nineteenth-century thought are nature, imagination and fancy. Two typical quotations will help us illustrate the use of these concepts. The first is from Johnson's *Prologue to Irene*:

> In Reason, Nature, Truth, he dares to trust:
> Ye Fops, be silent, and ye Wits, be just!

The second is from ch. XIII of *Biographia Literaria*, where Coleridge makes his famous distinction between fancy and imagination:

> The Imagination then, I consider either as primary, or secondary.
> The primary Imagination I hold to be the living Power and prime
> Agent of all human Perception, and as a repetition in the finite
> mind of the eternal act of creation in the infinite I AM. The
> secondary Imagination I consider as an echo of the former, co-
> existing with the conscious will, yet still as identical with the
> primary in the *kind* of its agency, and differing only in the
> *degree*, and in the *mode* of its operation. It dissolves, diffuses,
> dissipates, in order to re-create; or where this process is
> rendered impossible, yet still at all events it struggles to
> idealize and to unify. It is essentially *vital*, even as all
> objects (*as* objects) are essentially fixed and dead.
>
> Fancy, on the contrary, has no other counters to play with, but
> fixities and definites. The Fancy is indeed no other than a mode
> of Memory emancipated from the order of time and space; ... But
> equally with the ordinary memory the Fancy must receive all its
> materials ready made from the law of association.[12]

These two terms — fancy and imagination — will become all-pervading in
Romantic criticism. Coleridge claims to have first introduced the
distinction in England and Wordsworth also made use of the terms in his
Preface to the *Lyrical Ballads*. However, as the meaning he gave to fancy
and imagination was different from Coleridge's, the famous critical
controversy between them ensued. But this is not our concern here. What
concerns us is expressed in Wordsworth's description of the new poetry
contained in the *Lyrical Ballads*, that "the feeling therein developed gives
importance to the action and situation, and not the action and situation to
the feeling". It was indeed a new poetry, quite different from the popular
poetry of the day. And it is the new poetry which necessarily brought in its
wake the new criticism of the Romantics.

REFERENCES

1. *Essays Moral, Political, and Literary*, 2 vols., ed. T. H. Green and
    T. H. Grose (1882; Aalen: Scientia Verlag, rpt. 1964), Vol. I, p. 1.
    All references are to this edition and will be given in the body of the
    text.
2. *The Critical Opinions of Samuel Johnson*, compiled with an Introduction
    by J. E. Brown (New York: Russell & Russell, 1926, 1961). All
    references to Johnson's critical writings are to this work and will be
    given in the body of the text.
3. Thomas Rymer, *A Short View of Tragedy* (1692), in *Critical Works*, ed.
    Zimansky, pp. 164-169. For Voltaire, see "L'Appel à toutes les nations
    de l'Europe" (1761), in *Oeuvres Complètes*, ed. Moland, Vol. XXIV,
    pp. 193 ff. Voltaire replied to Johnson's censure in "Du théâtre
    anglais", *Dictionnaire Philosophique*, and in 1776 renewed the attack on
    Shakespeare in "Lettre à l'Académie francaise", Vol. XXX, pp. 349 ff.
    John Dennis, *An Essay on the Genius and Writings of Shakespeare* (1712),
    in *Works*, ed. Hooker, Vol. II, pp. 5-6.
4. Quoted in E. C. Mossner, *The Life of David Hume* (Oxford: Clarendon Press,
    1954; rpt. 1970), p. 377.
5. *Preface to Shakespeare*, in *English Critical Texts*, ed. D. J. Enright and
    E. De Chickera (London: Oxford Univ. Press, 1962, 1966), p. 145.

6. *Selected Essays from The Rambler, Adventurer and Idler*, ed. W. J. Bate
    (New Haven, London: Yale Univ. Press, 1968), p. 197.
7. In *The Great Critics*, ed. J. H. Smith and E. W. Parks (New York:
    W. W. Norton & Co. Inc., 1932, 1967), pp. 816–817.
8. *Selected Essays*, pp. 299–300.
9. *Critical Essays of the Seventeenth Century*, 3 vols., ed. J. E. Spingarn
    (1908; Bloomington, London: Indiana Univ. Press, 1968), Vol. II,
    pp. 117–118.
10. *Classical Literary Criticism*, ed. T. S. Dorsch (Penguin Books, 1965),
    pp. 62–63.
11. J. A. K. Thompson, *The Ethics of Aristotle* (Penguin Books, 1953, 1965),
    pp. 65–66.
12. Ed. J. Shawcross, 2 vols. (1907; Oxford Univ. Press, 1967), Vol. I,
    p. 202.

CHAPTER 5

Coleridge and the Rhetoric of Imagination

I

There can be no doubt that for the Romantics Imagination is the supreme and most encompassing of all value terms. It is the term most frequently used in all their critical writings, Fancy running a close second. But not so Reason, a term whose use and importance is gradually growing less. We need no statistical data to prove this: it is sufficient to open the writings of the Romantics at random, to realise that for them imagination is not only an aesthetic value term, but simply the highest value term there is, including the good, the beautiful and the true.

Whatever the individual differences in the particular views of Romantic poets and critics regarding imagination, fancy, feeling and reason may be, they are unimportant; what is important is the almost universal belief in the supremacy of the imagination for the real life of man and all human activities — not only the artistic, but also the moral, religious, social and personal. As J. Shawcross remarks in the Introduction to his edition of *Biographia Literaria*, "The Imagination thus appears allied to the moral consciousness; and art is the visible symbol of this relationship."[1] And although he is speaking only of Coleridge, his statement applies equally to all the Romantics.

Coleridge believed that imagination has an intrinsic and unalterable value, whose symbol is art in general and poetry in particular. However, being a poet himself, he knew that there is good and bad poetry, there are good and bad poets, as well as a great number of indifferent ones. He wanted therefore to find a standard for judging poetry, he wanted to discover some true, universal and unalterable principles which would enable the reader to distinguish between the good, the bad and the indifferent poems or poets. Already in 1811, as Payne Collier records in his *Diary*, "He means very soon, to give a series of lectures ... mainly upon Poetry, with a view to erect some standard by which all poets may be measured and ranked.... He thought something of this kind was very much needed, in order to settle people's notions of what was, or was not, good poetry, and who was, or was not a good poet" (liii, n. 1).

We see, therefore, that Coleridge's aim as a critic is no different from

that of his predecessors; in fact, no different from that of all great
critics, namely to discover and formulate some standard and principles
which would serve as effective instruments of criticism and evaluation. The
fact that he himself did not succeed in realising his intention in practice
is not our concern here. What concerns us is: first, his view of the end of
criticism and the rules of art; second, his definitions and use of the
concepts of Fancy and Imagination; and third, his critical analysis of some
poems and plays, i.e. his practical criticism. It is only then that we
shall be able to appraise Coleridge's real importance as a great modern
critic.

(a) The End of Criticism and the Rules of Art

In *Biographia Literaria*, ch. XVIII, Coleridge writes:

> The ultimate end of criticism is much more to establish the
> principles of writing, than to furnish *rules* how to pass judgement
> on what has been written by others; if indeed it were possible
> that the two could be separated. But if it be asked, by what
> principles the poet is to regulate his own style, if he do not
> adhere closely to the sort and order of words which he hears in
> the market, wake, high-road, or plough-field? I reply; by
> principles, the ignorance or neglect of which would convict him of
> being no poet, but a silly and presumptuous usurper of the name!
> By the principles of grammar, logic, psychology! In one word by
> such knowledge of the facts, material and spiritual, that most
> pertain to his art ..." (Vol. II, pp. 63-64).

When reading the passage carefully, we notice that Coleridge is using the
terms and phrases of criticism and rhetoric, e.g. "principles of writing",
"rules", "the sort and order of words", "principles of grammar, logic,
psychology" and knowledge appertaining to the art of poetry. In fact, he is
simply talking of those rules that pertain to the poet's and the critic's
art. We can call them linguistic, rhetorical, poetic rules, or rules of
writing and composition and, by extension, rules of criticism. For no poet,
as Coleridge says, can be regarded as a poet who is ignorant of such
elementary rules of language, just as no critic can be regarded as a critic
if he is ignorant of them. The poet, for instance, must know what words are
suitable to the portrayal of anger, jealousy or of any other passion and
emotion. And, moreover, he must also know what words are suitable for the
portrayal of different kinds, degrees and intensities of the various
passions, e.g. anger that is suppressed or indulged in, and so on.

It should be noticed that what Coleridge is trying to say is that the good
poet will be known by the language he uses in his description, portrayal or
representation of human passions and emotions. Coleridge knew from his own
experience that poetry is an art demanding the most precise craftsmanship.
How that craftsmanship is acquired is really beside the point: it may be
acquired by experience and observation, by an extensive knowledge of

different men and their manners, habits and ways of life; it may be acquired
by thought and meditation, by imagining certain situations and conditions,
just as much as by direct observation of actual situations and conditions.
The means is unimportant — it is only the end that counts. If, therefore,
Coleridge argues against observation and in favour of meditation as a way of
gaining knowledge of human nature in general, and the different manifesta-
tions of passions in particular, this does not disprove my contention:
namely, that behind all this, what Coleridge is really interested in is *not*
the different ways of acquiring this knowledge, but the ways of embodying it
in poetic language.

Coleridge explains that in a poet (or rather, in a true poet) the knowledge
of his craft becomes instinctive: he will know instinctively, or intuitively,
"what intermixture of conscious volition is natural to that state; and in
what instances such figures and colours of speech degenerate into mere
creatures of arbitrary purpose, cold technical devices of ornament or
connection" (Vol. II, p. 64). These "cold technical devices of ornament"
result from the mechanical application of external, arbitrary, codified
rules. But a real poet does not need them: for he creates his own rules
from within himself, and they grow together with, and are inseparable from,
the work of art in which they are embodied. In Coleridge's words, "Could a
rule be given from *without*, poetry would cease to be poetry, and sink into a
mechanical art.... The *rules* of Imagination are themselves the very powers
of growth and production" (Vol. II, p. 65).

In this passage Coleridge uses a number of psychological terms such as
"field of vision", "inward experience", "a clearer intuition", "the true
sources of genial discrimination", "intermixture of conscious volition",
"the power of imagination" (Vol. II, pp. 64–65). But in fact he only uses
them in order to give greater weight to what he has been saying before,
namely: that the good poet will know what figures and colours of speech are
proper or natural for the different characters, states, situations, passions
and feelings presented. Poets who use artificial forms of speech and
unnatural metaphors are simply bad poets.

Coleridge proceeds to illustrate the difference between good and bad poetic
language by concrete examples. Thus Donne's apostrophe to the Sun in the
second stanza of his "Progress of the Soul" is good, appropriate,
legitimate. On the other hand, such poems as the Odes to Jealousy, to Hope,
to Oblivion and the like (in Dodsley's *A Collection of Poems*, published in
1748 and frequently reprinted) are bad. Such poems are mechanical, not
organic; and their authors are clearly writing according to external,
mechanical rules, not according to internal, organic ones; they have neither
genius, talent, experience, observation, nor the capacity for meditation and
contemplation.

Throughout the whole chapter, Coleridge passes imperceptibly from one
language level to another: from an analysis of poetic language and its
devices to an analysis of the poet's mental capacities. And this is the
reason why most modern commentators have only seized on one aspect of
Coleridge's criticism to the detriment of the others. They have concentrated their attention on a meticulous analysis, exposition and interpretation of his theory of the imagination, without paying sufficient
attention to his analysis of poetic discourse and rhetorical devices. They
have praised Coleridge for his philosophical, theoretical and psychological
criticism, rather than for his particular critical analyses. But it is the
practical or applied criticism that makes him the great critic he is, rather
than his theoretical excursuses into German idealistic philosophy and

Kantian aesthetics.

Condemning the rhetorical devices of Cowley's *Pindaric Odes*, Coleridge maintains that good sense and a moderate insight into the human mind would be sufficient to prove that such language and such combinations as Cowley's are the products of neither fancy nor imagination, since "their operation consists in the excitement of surprise by the juxta-position and *apparent* reconciliation of widely different or incompatible things" (Vol. II, pp. 67-68). We should remember that the real reconciliation of opposites is for Coleridge the true mark of imagination.

Coleridge's use of fancy and imagination in this passage is, I think, superfluous. For what is he really saying except that the good poet knows how to use language and what language is proper to the different genres of poetry? All the poet needs to know are the materials and tools of his craft: language and its rules and uses, and what he wants to make — a poem, a play, a story, a novel, a fairy-tale, and so on. As Coleridge puts it in his essay "On Poesy or Art", the poet "must out of his own mind create forms according to the severe laws of the intellect" (Vol. II, p. 258). He must therefore never forget that, like all the arts, poetry too has its laws, rules, order and organisation. Or, as he says elsewhere, "No work of genius dare want its appropriate form; neither indeed is there any danger of this. As it must not, so neither can it, be lawless! For it is even this that constitutes it genius — the power of acting creatively under laws of its own creation" (Raysor, Vol. I, pp. 197-198).

Coleridge concludes chapter XVIII with the repeated assertion that the only rule and guidance the poet needs are to be deduced in his own mind "from considerations of grammar, logic, and the truth and nature of things, confirmed by the authority of works, whose fame is not of ONE country nor of ONE age" (Vol. II, p. 68).

We see that Coleridge here agrees with all the critics before him that the great works of art are those that have stood the test of time; and that the great poets are those who know their craft: who know to use language to its utmost limits, so that by their skilful use of it they continually widen its range, and hence the range of our awareness. And finally, that, because the poet is the master of language, he can make us aware of those things and aspects of things — whether external or internal — which we couldn't know before, having no words to describe and express them. Coleridge's definition of poetry as "The best words in the best order" (and not in terms of imagination or fancy) shows him to belong to the great tradition of English criticism. In spite of his metaphysical and psychological terminology and theories, which make his meaning ambiguous and therefore capable of being variously interpreted according to the philosophical and psychological preferences of the commentator, Coleridge is first and foremost a critic whose concern is language, particularly the language of poetry, to the analysis and understanding of which he has devoted the most important part of his *Biographia*, his *Shakespearean Criticism*, his Lectures, marginalia, notebooks and critical fragments.

It should be emphasised that Coleridge retained many critical terms and views of his neoclassical predecessors, and that in spite of his introduction of new, psychological terms and concepts into his criticism. His continuation of the critical tradition can be seen, for example, in his views of the end of criticism and the function of the critic, which closely resemble those of such neoclassical critics as Johnson and Addison. Johnson,

writing in the *Rambler 176*, observes that "The eye of the intellect, like
that of the body, is not equally perfect in all, nor equally adapted in any
to all objects; the end of criticism is to supply its defects; rules are
the instruments of mental vision, which may indeed assist our faculties when
properly used but produce confusion and obscurity by unskillful application"
(Brown, p. 49).

We know that Johnson ranked criticism as a subordinate and instrumental art
(cf. *Rambler 208*). The critic, therefore, has a definite task to fulfil:
he should help the reader see and understand what he could not have done
without his professional help. Furthermore, Johnson believes that the true
critic will reveal everything about the work he is criticising, both its
beauties *and* its faults, for, as he writes in the *Rambler 93*, "the duty of
criticism is neither to depreciate, nor dignify by partial representations,
but to hold out the light of reason, whatever it may discover ..." (Brown,
p. 48). Addison, on the other hand, believed that it is one of the
characteristics of the true critic to point out beauties rather than faults.

In ch. III of the *Biographia*, writing about the principles of modern
criticism, Coleridge states his conviction that

> ... till reviews are conducted on far other principles, and with
> far other motives; till in the place of arbitrary dictation and
> petulant sneers, the reviewers support their decisions by
> reference to *fixed canons of criticism*, previously established and
> deduced from the nature of man; reflecting minds will pronounce it
> arrogance in them to announce themselves to men of letters, as the
> guides of their taste and judgement. To the purchaser and mere
> reader it is, at all events, an injustice. He who tells me that
> there are *defects* in a new work, tells me nothing which I should
> not have taken for granted without his information. But he, who
> points out and elucidates the *beauties* of an original work, does
> indeed give me interesting information, such as experience would
> not have authorized me in anticipating" (Vol. I, p. 44).

It is important to note that Coleridge fully agrees with the views of
Johnson and Addison quoted above. Furthermore, given the fact that he
speaks of "fixed canons of criticism" and the defects and beauties of a
concrete work of literature, he does not even mention fancy and imagination.
Where concrete works of art are in question, where Coleridge refers to
canons, principles, rules and standards which, as we have seen earlier,
belong to the field of grammar, syntax, logic and the structure of language,
the use of psychological concepts would not be very helpful. In addition,
it must be noted that Coleridge does not even mention in the present
instance such things as the mental make-up of the poet or the processes of
poetic creation. But he does mention such prosaic, down-to-earth matters as
"information", which the critic can give the reader, by elucidating the
beauties of the work: information which the reader (in this case Coleridge
himself) will be happy to receive from him, because, as is implied, he
wouldn't have been able to discover it by himself.

In ch. II, Coleridge gives us an illuminating illustration of his method as
a practical critic. And from this one example we can learn more about how
a good critic actually works than from many of Coleridge's theoretical
speculations on the end of criticism in general. He reports that in the
course of one of his public Lectures he contrasted Pope's original poems,
his Satires and Essays, with his translation of Homer. He shows that Pope
is a good poet in the former, a bad poet in the latter; and he does it only

by comparing his language, which is natural in his own poetry, but
artificial in his translation. After pointing out "the almost faultless
position and choice of words" in Pope's original compositions, he then turns
to his translation of Homer. Taking a well-known passage of the *Iliad*,
Book VIII, he proceeds to analyse it sentence by sentence, and almost word
by word. The effect on the audience was immediately visible. And, at the
end of the lecture, many people acknowledged that their whole view of the
poem was radically changed: where before they had only blindly admired, they
now knew that their admiration was unjustified; and they wondered how they
had not recognised earlier that this was not poetic diction, but only
pseudo-poetic (Vol. I, pp. 26–27n).

There are several points to be noted in this passage: first, and most
important, that Coleridge is here clearly doing the kind of close verbal
analysis which was to become the most widespread critical method of our time;
second, that the ordinary reader, if left completely to himself, is unable
to do the work of the professional critic (it must be remarked in passing
that Coleridge's audience consisted of "enlightened and highly educated
persons"); and finally, that Coleridge never once mentions such things as
Pope's lack of imagination or fancy: all he needs to do in order to make his
audience *see* for themselves is to show them where to look; once they are
told that it is the way the poet uses his words and the kind of words he
uses that make him a good or a bad poet, they can then go on by themselves.
And this again is a characteristic of twentieth-century criticism and
critical method.

It is interesting to compare what Coleridge says about the end of criticism,
the different types of critic and the function of the critic with Eliot's
views on these matters. In one of his last critical essays, "The Frontiers
of Criticism" (1956), Eliot first of all draws attention to the transfor-
mation of criticism which began with Coleridge "but which has proceeded
with greater acceleration during the last twenty-five years". There is a
great variety of criticism today, but yet Eliot wonders whether there is not
some common ground amidst all this variety. He believes there is, namely
their common aim "to promote the understanding and enjoyment of literature".
If this is so, then the critic's task is to help his readers attain this
aim. In addition, "the critic may on occasion be called to condemn the
second-rate and expose the fraudulent: though that duty is secondary to the
duty of discriminating praise of what is praiseworthy". Eliot enlarges on
what he means by understanding a poem: "To understand a poem comes to the
same thing as to enjoy it for the right reasons." The literary critic is
he who can help the reader understand poetry and literature for the right
reasons. But, like the poet himself, the critic too must have other
interests beside literature: "for the literary critic is not merely a
technical expert, who has learned the rules to be observed by the writers he
criticizes: the critic must be the whole man, a man with convictions and
principles, and of knowledge and experience of life".

Eliot concludes with some final remarks about which critic seems to him most
helpful: "So the critic to whom I am most grateful is the one who can make
me look at something I have never looked at before, or looked at only with
eyes clouded with prejudice, set me face to face with it and then leave me
alone with it. From that point, I must rely upon my sensibility, intelli-
gence, and capacity for wisdom."[3]

This is exactly what Coleridge did with his enlightened and highly educated
audience during his lectures. Thus, not only with regard to their views of
the end of criticism and the function of the critic, but also with regard to

critical methods, is there great similarity between Coleridge and Eliot.

In his examination of the "Principles of Modern Criticism" in ch. III, Coleridge attacks the false methods of many contemporary critics. In chs. II and III he singles out for severe denunciation the prevalent evil of anonymous reviewers and critics, writing their virulent attacks against new poets and new poetry (e.g. of Southey, Coleridge and Wordsworth), without running the danger of their victims' answering back, simply because they do not know who those critics are. Coleridge illustrates to what lengths those "quacks in criticism" would go: their method was to single out the defects and accidental failures or some faulty passages in the author they were reviewing and then go on to enlarge on them endlessly. In *Anima Poetae* (1803), Coleridge calls this kind of criticism "the head-dimming, heart-damping principle of judging a work by its defects, not its beauties" (Vol. I, p. 220). Using Andrew Marvell's phrase, he calls these anonymous critics "synodical individuals", who speak of themselves in the plural as if they were kings.

Coleridge's repeated attacks against the anonymous reviewers of his day constitutes a highly significant feature of the *Biographia*. Not so much in what it tells us about Coleridge himself, but in pointing to an important sociological fact: critics appear to be numerous; they have become a power to be reckoned with — by writers, publishers and the public. They have a definite function, a status and a language of their own. They seem to have become a separate group, still loosely connected to the republic of letters, but already independent of it. They seem aware of themselves as a power, and they expect others to acknowledge them as such. In fact, they have become a corporate body of littérateurs, in modern terms a pressure group. We recall Johnson's satire of Dick Minim, the brewer's apprentice who turned critic by using the fashionable cant phrases of his day (*Idler 60,61*). But there is a difference between Dick Minim and the anonymous critics and reviewers of Coleridge's day: Dick Minim is at least inoffensive; he doesn't have the necessary intellect and virulence which those "critical quacks" apparently possessed.

We can conclude, therefore, that by the beginning of the nineteenth century criticism as an independent discipline has definitely come of age. The ever-growing reading public (which, by the way, Coleridge also singles out for special attack as not being interested in literature *per se*, but only as a pastime or amusement, see for instance Vol. I, p. 34n); the growing number of poets, novelists, essayists, historians, journalists, shows that quantity was beginning to change the quality of the republic of letters. A lowering of the standard of tastes, a vulgarisation, and a popularisation of literature was inevitable; and the second-rate critics of the numerous little reviews and publications contributed their share.

But also in the more important periodicals such as the *Edinburgh Review*, whose editor was Jeffrey, there were critics who, like Jeffrey, were "taking it for granted that the critic is, by virtue of his office, superior to every person he chooses to summon before him" (Vol. I, p. 216n). And these critics apparently had the power to make or break a reputation.

There is no doubt that criticism had become an independent discipline, with a territory, a population, a constitution (though unwritten), a terminology and rules of its own. Synodical individuals, critical quacks and dictators abounded, and so, of course, did the Dick Minims. But, as is only to be expected, the true critics, as always, were rare. Coleridge, however, was undoubtedly one of those rare true critics.

(b) On Fancy and Imagination

The two concepts of Fancy and Imagination which, as Coleridge tells us, he was the first to use as distinct concepts in English criticism, are so much part of our current critical terminology that we accept them unquestioningly as referring to two distinct mental capacities; and furthermore, that these two distinct mental capacities (or "faculties" as Coleridge calls them) are really there, in our or the poet's mind, for the words to refer to. It is worth our while to re-examine these concepts — their origin, meaning, use and varying definitions in Coleridge's work.

In ch. IV Coleridge tells us how he first came to think of fancy and imagination as two distinct concepts. It is important that we know the exact genesis of these terms, in order to be able to decide about their validity — whether linguistic or psychological. For we shall see that, whereas their origin is linguistic, the use to which Coleridge and other psychological critics after him put it is primarily psychological.

Coleridge recalls that, having read and admired a manuscript poem of Wordsworth (afterwards incorporated in *Guilt and Sorrow*) and *felt* its excellence, he immediately tried to *understand* it: "Repeated meditations led me first to suspect (and a more intimate analysis of the human faculties, their appropriate marks, functions, and effects matured my conjecture into full conviction,) that fancy and imagination were two distinct and widely different faculties, instead of being, according to the general belief, either two names with one meaning, or, at furthest, the lower and higher degree of one and the same power" (Vol. I, pp. 60-61). After a short disquisition on the difference between the Greek *Phantasia* and the Latin *Imaginatio*, Coleridge continues:

> The first and most important point to be proved is, that two conceptions perfectly distinct are confused under one and the same word, and (this done) to appropriate that word exclusively to one meaning, and the synonyme (should there be one) to the other. But if (as will be often the case in the arts and sciences) no synonyme exists, we must either invent or borrow a word. In the present instance the appropriation has already begun, and been legitimated in the derivative adjective: Milton had a highly *imaginative*, Cowley a very *fanciful* mind" (Vol. I, pp. 61-62).

It is this last sentence which is the most important, because it shows us
that Coleridge's use of these two adjectives — imaginative and fanciful —
is not at all descriptive, as he implies, but clearly evaluative. In fact,
as Eliot has rightly remarked, "the difference between imagination and
fancy amounts in practice to no more than the difference between good and
bad poetry".[4]

Let us follow up this distinction between description and evaluation, or
between descriptive and evaluative terms and uses, a little more closely.
Thus, when Coleridge says that Milton had a highly imaginative mind, Cowley
a very fanciful one, we are justified in asking "How does he know?" And the
only possible answer is that Coleridge knows about these two poets' minds
only by inference from their poetry. In fact, he cannot show us how their
minds worked except by quoting some lines from their poems in order to show
concretely the difference between a fanciful and an imaginative mind and
poet. Unfortunately, Coleridge does not follow up his earlier statement
with a concrete illustration from Cowley's and Milton's poems. In fact,
although there are a number of references to Cowley's Latin Poems, his
translation of Pindar and his school of poetry, there is not a single
quotation to support Coleridge's contention that Cowley's mind and his
poetry are fanciful. As to Milton's poetry, we have to wait till the
penultimate chapter of the *Biographia*, ch. XXII, for a concrete illustration
from Milton's poetry which is described as having imaginative power.

Contrasting Wordsworth's *The Excursion* with its "minute accuracy in the
painting of local imagery" with Milton's poetic painting, Coleridge states
that the essential difference between the imaginative and the fanciful is a
difference of structure and effect: a poem which is fanciful will have one
kind of effect on the reader, a poem which is imaginative quite another.
The former demands from the reader an effort in order to understand it; the
latter is immediately and effortlessly understood. When reading certain
fanciful lines of *The Excursion*, for example, we seem "to be taking the
pieces of a dissected map out of its box. We first look at one part, and
then at another, then join and dove-tail them; and when the successive acts
of attention have been completed, there is a retrogressive effort of mind to
behold it as a whole" (Vol. II, p. 102). When reading Milton's description
of the fig tree in *Paradise Lost*, 9. 1100, on the other hand, there is
"such co-presence of the whole picture flash'd at once upon the eye, as the
sun paints in a camera obscura" (Vol. II, p. 103) that Coleridge concludes
it is imaginative creation, and not mere fanciful painting.

In this illustration of the difference between imagination and fancy or
between imaginative and fanciful, Coleridge uses the two terms to refer to
three different things: the poet, the poem and the reader. Starting from
the effects the poem has on the reader (in this case Coleridge himself), the
qualities of the poem and the qualities of the poet are inferred by him to
be such and such. When Coleridge states that "The poet should paint to the
imagination, not to the fancy", he of course means the imagination and
fancy of the reader. We then get something like this: the imaginative poet
(Milton) is he who writes an imaginative poem addressed to the imagination
of the reader; the fanciful poet (Wordsworth in *The Excursion*) is he who
writes a fanciful poem addressed to the fancy of the reader. But what is of
interest to the literary critic is neither the mental make-up of the poet
nor the different effects the poem may have on different readers at different times. What interests him is the poem itself, its images, qualities,
structure, meaning, complexity and so on. From the above-quoted illustration of the difference between imagination and fancy we do not learn very
much about the respective two poems. To do so we have to turn to other,

more precise and more analytical illustrations of this difference.

Coleridge illustrates the difference between imagination and fancy by
quoting two lines from two plays. The first is from Otway's *Venice
Preserved*, Act V:

> "Lutes, lobsters, seas of milk, and ships of amber"

and the second from *King Lear*, Act III, scene 4, where Lear exclaims:

> "What! have his daughters brought him to this pass?"

It should be noticed that Coleridge misquotes Otway's line, which reads:
"Lutes, laurels, seas of milk, and ships of amber", which makes quite a
difference. Otway's line is given as an example of fancy, Shakespeare's as
an example of imagination, but Coleridge does not justify his description or
enlarge on it.

Furthermore, both lines are quoted out of context, and surely cannot be made
to carry all the fanciful or imaginative weight of the whole passage or
scene in which they occur. By calling these two lines illustrations of the
workings of fancy and imagination respectively, Coleridge is already
weighting his evidence: for we know that imagination is regarded by him, by
all the Romantic poets and even by us as higher in the scale of "mental
faculties" than fancy. And the same is true of works called imaginative or
fanciful. So, by calling one poet, or one poem, or even a single line
"imaginative" and the other "fanciful", Coleridge already implies that the
former is good, the latter not so good, or even bad. Although we do not
know how we would judge the whole scene of Otway and Shakespeare (though we
are familiar with the latter, and *know* it is good), we can nevertheless
analyse the two lines. And we find that Otway's original line (not as mis-
quoted by Coleridge) strikes us as rather strange: it is not clear what the
logical connection or the poetic association between lutes, laurels, seas of
milk and ships of amber can possibly be; on the other hand, taking Lear's
line in isolation, it is not at all clear why it should be described as
highly imaginative. We can suppose this same question put to a friend in
distress, and we would not then be struck by its dramatic and imaginative
quality — possibly only by its expressing human sympathy.

Further light on the difference between fancy and imagination or, as
Coleridge calls them, "the assimilative" and "the modifying faculties"
(Vol. II, p. 19), is thrown by Coleridge's Notebook No.25, in a section
entitled "Shakespeare's Poetry" (and probably belonging to the Lectures on
Shakespeare of 1808). Coleridge illustrates from Shakespeare's poetry and
drama what he means by fancy and imagination. He writes that "we have shown
that he possessed fancy, considered as the faculty of bringing together
[images dissimilar in the main by some one point or more of likeness
distinguished].

> Full gently now she takes him by the hand,
> A lily prison'd in a gaol of snow,
> Or ivory in an alabaster band;
> So white a friend engirts so white a foe.
> > (*Venus and Adonis*, 361-364)"

Whereas in the earlier example of fancy we could not discover any common
point between the dissimilar images (lutes, laurels, seas of milk and ships
of amber), here, at all events, there is at least the one common quality of

whiteness; and possibly the additional quality of coldness, generally associated with lilies, snow, ivory and alabaster. This enumeration of different images, this contingent association or assimilation, makes neither for harmony and fusion nor for real unity. This can be done only by imagination, "or the power by which one image or feeling is made to modify many others and by a sort of *fusion to force many into one*" (Raysor, Vol. I, p. 188). It is at this point that Coleridge again brings in *King Lear* as a supreme example of Shakespeare's imagination, that faculty of "producing out of many things, as they would have appeared in the description of an ordinary mind, described slowly and in unimpassioned succession, a oneness, even as nature, the greatest of poets, acts upon us when we open our eyes upon an extended prospect". The mark of fancy is multiplicity, the mark of imagination is unity.

Coleridge's most extended analysis of imaginative unity is shown in two lines from *Venus and Adonis* describing "the flight of Adonis from the enamoured goddess in the dusk of the evening —

> Look! how a bright star shooteth from the sky,
> So glides he in the night from Venus' eye.
>   (*Venus and Adonis*, 815-816)"

Coleridge comments enthusiastically: "How many images and feelings are here brought together without effort and without discord — the beauty of Adonis — the rapidity of his flight — the yearning yet hopelessness of the enamoured gazer — and a shadowy ideal character thrown over the whole" (Raysor, Vol. I, pp. 188-189).

In another draft of the same lecture, and coming from the same notebook, Coleridge succinctly defines Imagination as the "power of modifying one image or feeling by the precedent or following ones" and "of combining many circumstances into one moment of thought to produce that ultimate end of human thought and human feeling, unity, and thereby the reduction of the spirit to its principle and fountain, who alone is truly *One*" (Raysor, Vol. I, pp. 191-192).

From all the preceding descriptions, definitions and illustrations of the workings of Imagination, we see that its essential characteristic is its power of reducing variety to unity. As Coleridge puts it at the end of ch. XIII, the Secondary Imagination, or esemplastic power, "dissolves, diffuses, dissipates, in order to recreate; or where this process is rendered impossible, yet still at all events it struggles to idealize and to unify. It is essentially *vital*, even as all objects (*as* objects) are essentially fixed and dead" (Vol. I, p. 202). Fancy, on the other hand, does not have this power: it leaves things more or less as it finds them. In fact, it "has not other counters to play with, but fixities and definites. The Fancy is indeed no other than a mode of Memory emancipated from the order of time and space...." (Ibid.)

From the foregoing examination of Coleridge's theory of the Imagination, and of his views regarding some of the differences between Imagination and Fancy, it is clear that he assumes the human mind to be made up of separate faculties (whatever Shawcross may say to the contrary).[5] As he himself tells us in an unpublished "Letter on Plagiarism", it was Kant who had taught him "to treat every subject in reference to the operation of the mental faculties to which it specially appertains, and to commence by the cautious discrimination of what is essential, i.e. explicable by the mere consideration of the faculties in themselves, from what is empirical, i.e.

the modifying or disturbing forces of time, place, and circumstances"
(Raysor, Vol. II, p. 189).

But, whereas for a metaphysician or a psychologist an interest in the
operation of the various mental faculties may be enough, this is not the
case for a literary critic: his interest is primarily empirical, i.e. in the
concrete works of art, the poems, plays, novels and short stories he
criticises and appraises. If, therefore, we are right in regarding
Coleridge as one of the greatest English critics — if not the greatest —
then the grounds for such an evaluation cannot be his philosophical and
psychological theories only, but also, and more importantly, his practical
literary criticism. His greatness lies not in his theory of the
imagination, not in his deep psychological analyses of Shakespearean
characters and their motives (for there are many other good psychological
critics), but, above all, in his analysis of the verbal and rhetorical
devices by means of which these characters are created and embodied. In
sum, it is in Coleridge's extraordinary sensitivity to language in which his
greatness, both as poet and critic, finally lies.

To sum up: Coleridge uses the terms fancy and imagination and their cognates
fanciful and imaginative as blanket terms, referring at times to poems, at
others to the minds of poets: i.e. the use of these terms is stretched from
the description of linguistic characteristics exhibited by particular poems,
to that of mental faculties. Moreover, Coleridge's distinction between
fancy and imagination is not at all clear cut, definite and homogenous. In
fact, these different terms are not descriptive at all, but evaluative,
being synonymous for good and not so good (or bad).

Already in the very first chapter of the *Biographia*, recalling his school-
days in the grammar school, Christ's Hospital, under its scholarly head-
master, the Rev. James Bowyer, Coleridge tells us that he "learnt from him,
that Poetry, even that of the loftiest and seemingly, that of the wildest
odes, had a logic of its own, as severe as that of science; and more
difficult, because more subtle, more complex, and dependent on more, and
more fugitive causes" (Vol. I, pp. 4-5).

This is clearly a passage of great importance: it shows that from his
earliest age Coleridge was trained in the technique of *explication de texte*,
i.e. an exact explication of classical and modern texts; and he was taught
to assign great value to all the verbal and rhetorical devices used by
ancient and modern tragic poets. This early training in language and
rhetoric seems to have been so well absorbed by him that later, when he
himself became a critic, especially a Shakespearean critic, it had become
almost instinctive. So that, as I suggested earlier, no amount of German
idealistic philosophy and aesthetics could obstruct Coleridge from doing
practical criticism of Shakespeare's individual plays. And it is, after all,
by his practical criticism that the critic shows himself for what he
really is — not in his theoretical speculations.

When, therefore, Coleridge observes that there is a logic of poetry as
severe as that of science, a logic which is even more difficult, subtle and
complex than that of science, what he probably means is that there is a
logic of language. And it is *because* language itself has a definite
logical structure, expressed in its rules of grammar and syntax, that we are
led to say that, for instance, science has a logic, and poetry a logic of
its own. Logic means the way terms are interconnected and interrelated.
And this interconnection and interrelation of terms is guided by rules,
varying in their definiteness and explicitness (according to the kind of

discourse to which they pertain).

Coleridge fully agrees with his old master who would say that "In the truly great poets, ... there is a reason assignable, not only for every word, but for the position of every word; ..." (Vol. I, p. 4). And the implication is that just as the great poets know wherein consists the peculiar fitness of the words they use, in just the order they occur in, so the great critic is also able to assign the right reason for the kind and order of the words in their respective poetic or dramatic contexts. (Although we are dealing here with poetry and not with fiction, it is worth while to recall at this point what Edmund Wilson says in his essay on Marcel Proust. Although at first we find that there is no logical connection between the different elements of *A la Recherche du Temps Perdu*, later we discover that "It has its harmony, development and logic, but they are the harmony, development and logic of the unconscious."[6] Thus not only is there a logic of poetry as distinct from the logic of science, but there is also a logic of the unconscious as distinct from the logic of the conscious.)

Coleridge further tells us how he was trained to distinguish between good poetry and bad or mediocre poetry by the same verbal analysis of different poems and poets. His master taught him to show "no mercy to phrase, metaphor, or image, unsupported by sound sense, or where the same sense might have been conveyed with equal force and dignity in plainer words. Lute, harp, and lyre, muse, muses and inspirations, Pegasus, Parnassus, and Hippocrene were all an abomination to him." There follows a sentence (italicised by Coleridge for greater emphasis) which is so dramatically vivid that we seem to see and hear the Rev. Bowyer himself sternly admonishing his class: *"Harp? Harp? Lyre? Pen and ink, boy, you mean! Muse, boy, Muse? Your Nurse's daughter, you mean! Pierian spring? Oh aye! the cloister-pump, I suppose!"* (Vol. I, p. 5).

The whole passage calls to mind a very similar one in Hobbes's *Answer to Davenant*, where he expresses his disapproval of the use of fictions, meta-morphoses and the supernatural in modern poetry, while approving it in the ancient. I suggested that this criticism is justified by the different logical implications or commitment of the different languages, the Greek and the English. The same is true of Bowyer's severe criticism of the "poetic diction" of eighteenth-century poetry, i.e. of Pope and his followers. It was characterised by certain introductions, similes and examples which had become completely stereotyped; and by "certain well known and ever returning phrases, both introductory and transitional, including a large assortment of modest egoisms, and flattering illeisms", that left no place for originality of thought, feeling and expression. It was a poetry which seemed to Coleridge "characterized not so much by poetic thoughts, as by thoughts *translated* into the language of poetry" (Vol. I, p. 11). He found, however, that this poetry too had a logic of its own, but, in contrast to the great poetry from Shakespeare to Cowley, it did not have a logic of poetry, but a "logic of wit, conveyed in smooth and strong epigrammatic couplets, as its *form*".

It is clear from the foregoing that for Coleridge there is no separation between content and form, matter and manner, thought and diction in poetry. He treats them as one, or, as he was fond of saying, as an organic unity. His metaphor for Augustan poetry is significant — "the whole was as it were a sorites, or, if I may exchange a logical for a grammatical metaphor, a *conjunction disjunctive*, of epigrams" (Vol. I, p. 11).

If we compare Coleridge's expressions "the logic of poetry", "the logic of wit", "poetic thoughts", "thoughts translated into the language of poetry" with Eliot's expressions "unified sensibility" and "dissociation of sensibility" used in his essay "The Metaphysical Poets", we realise that both critics are using different expressions for describing the same things. What both of them are trying to convey by these expressions are the qualities of great poetry and the qualities of poetry which may be good, but which can never attain to the poetry of the highest kind. In addition, these descriptive phrases are at the same time evaluative, so that when Coleridge says that Shakespeare, Donne and Milton are great poets, he means that their poetry has such a strong logical structure "that it would be scarcely more difficult to push a stone out from the pyramids with the bare hand, than to alter a word, or the position of a word, in Milton and Shakespeare in their most important works at least), without making the author say something else, or something worse, than he does say" (Vol. I, p. 15).

But this is not the case with lesser poetry, which does not possess this organic unity, this unity as of a living organism. The logic of wit which Augustan poetry exhibits is, as Coleridge implies, of a different and lower kind than the logic of great poetry; it is a logic more appropriate to prose than to poetry. Therefore Coleridge says that it seems like a translation, not a true creation, something artificial, unnatural, discursive, argumentative; something, in short, made not grown. (In his essay "On Poesy or Art", Coleridge expresses it thus: "Remember that there is a difference between form as proceeding, and shape as superimposed — the latter is either the death or the imprisonment of the thing; — the former is its self-witnessing and self-effected sphere of agency" [Vol. II, p. 262]).

According to Eliot, a dissociation of sensibility set in as early as the seventeenth century, which divided poetry into two different kinds: the poetry of feeling of the Romantics and the reflective poetry of Tennyson and Browning, of the Victorians. But neither kind can attain the highest degree of poetry, which "is a direct sensuous apprehension of thought, or a re-creation of thought into feeling, ...".[7] There is, I suggest, great similarity between Eliot's "unified sensibility" and Coleridge's organic unity as qualities of great poetry.

(c) Coleridge as a Practical Critic

Coleridge is generally regarded as one of the three great English critics, the other two being Johnson and Arnold. But, whereas all agree that he is a great critic, no one seems to know in what exactly his greatness consists. Many theorists describe him as a philosophical or theoretical critic and proceed to trace in detail the influence of German idealistic philosophy on Coleridge's various writings; they attach great importance to his similarities to and differences from such philosophers as Kant, Fichte, the Schellings, and aestheticians like Richter and Schiller. This is, for instance, the method adopted by J. Shawcross in his long Introduction to his edition of *Biographia Literaria* and of M. H. Abrams in *The Mirror and the Lamp*[8] (though he also gives much attention to the differences between Coleridge's theory of the Imagination as an organism and Hartley's mechanical theory of associationism). These modern commentators treat Coleridge first of all as a theoretical critic, whose practice must be shown and seen as deriving from his theory, and will therefore be more easily understood (as being subsumable under definite general theoretical principles).

This whole approach derives partly from Coleridge's own views and pronouncements, for, as he tells us, "Metaphysics, poetry and facts of mind, are my darling studies." Modern critics, therefore, following Coleridge's lead, have concentrated their exposition and interpretation of Coleridge's criticism under these three heads: philosophy, psychology and poetry, giving most of their attention to the first two at the expense of the third. But it is surely the third which is crucial for any literary critic: that is, we shall regard him as a great critic not necessarily because he has a good theory of criticism (or of poetry) but because he is a good practical critic. If, that is, his analysis of specific works and of specific poets is such that it reveals these works in a new light, if he makes us see things, aspects, truths, which we would not have been able to discover for ourselves: in short, if he increases our understanding and enjoyment of literary works.

It is on ch. XIV of the *Biographia* that much of Coleridge's fame as a critic rests — because in it he gives his famous philosophic definitions of a poem, of poetry and a poet, as well as illustrations of the workings of the Imagination. It is here that Coleridge asserts that imagination both apprehends the essences of things and recreates them in sensible form: he does this by quoting Sir John Davies's poem *Nosce Teipsum*, which, though addressed to the soul, Coleridge applies to the poetic imagination. After expressing his disagreement with Wordsworth's theory of the imagination as set out in his earlier Prefaces to the *Lyrical Ballads* of 1800 and 1802, Coleridge observes that "With many parts of this preface in the sense attributed to them, and which the words undoubtedly seem to authorize, I never concurred; but on the contrary objected to them as erroneous in principle, and as contradictory ... to the author's own practice in the greatest number of the poems themselves" (Vol. II, pp. 7-8).

The same is true *mutatis mutandis* of Coleridge himself. And, just as he rejected Wordsworth's theory of the imagination while regarding his poetry as a living embodiment of the poetic imagination, we can reject his literary theory, garbed as it is in the metaphysical terminology of transcendental idealism, while regarding his practical criticism of Wordsworth, Shakespeare, Donne and various aspects of the drama (in his *Shakespearean Criticism*) as important in its own right and still relevant today. I shall devote this chapter to an examination of some aspects of Coleridge's practical criticism, paying special attention to his criteria of literary excellence and his theory and illustration of good poetic language.

I have already commented on Coleridge's various definitions of Fancy and Imagination and noted that whenever he uses these two words and their cognates it is in fact as synonyms for good and not so good. Accepting as he does the faculty psychology of mental activities, with a clear hierarchy of faculties going from the lowest to the highest, i.e. from mere passive perception to god-like creation, there will clearly be a parallel hierarchy of poets and of poems: those poets who possess poetic imagination will be placed at the top, those who possess only fancy at the bottom; and similarly, those poems which exhibit these two different faculties in different degrees will be placed on the appropriate rungs of the scale.

It is worth recalling at this point that Coleridge regarded fancy, understanding and empirical choice as the lower faculties; imagination, reason and will as the higher ones. Already in ch. I he tells us that "According to the faculty or source, from which the pleasure given by any poem or passage was derived, I estimated the merit of such poem or passage" (Vol. I, p. 14); and in ch. XIV he repeats his belief in a hierarchy of human faculties when he writes that "The poet, described in *ideal* perfection, brings the whole soul of man into activity, with the subordination of its faculties to each other, according to their relative worth and dignity" (Vol. II, p. 12).[9]

Since ch. XXII is the most extended practical analysis of one poet in the *Biographia*, it is worth examining it in some detail. The title itself is significant and gives us its content: "The characteristic defects of Wordsworth's poetry, with the principles from which the judgment, that they are defects, is deduced — Their proportion to the beauties — For the greatest part characteristic of his theory only." I shall concentrate only on the beauties or virtues of Wordsworth's poetry because it is here, if anywhere, that Coleridge will show us concretely how imagination works in practice.

The five defects of Wordsworth's poems are: inconstancy of style, matter-of-factness (or "a laborious minuteness" of details and the accidental), a predilection of the dramatic form, verbal bombast (or prolixity and repetition) and mental bombast. In this long chapter Coleridge devotes the whole first half to an examination of these defects, and he does so by adducing concrete examples from Wordsworth's poetry. In fact, in this first

part we find very little theoretical generalisations, except the remark that
"The poet should paint to the imagination, not to the fancy" (Vol. II,
p. 102). And although he does not say so, Coleridge assumes that all
Wordsworth's defects spring from his fancy, which is "recondite" or without
grace. However, since his defects are only occasional, they have not the
power to detract from "his depth of feeling and his imaginative power"
(Vol. II, p. 104), or, in other words, from his greatness.

Be it remarked that of the five defects only one, the fifth, deals with the
subject, while all the other four deal with style. Having examined the
defects of some of Wordsworth's poems, Coleridge proceeds to examine their
virtues, which are six: a grammatical and logical purity of language (or a
perfect appropriateness of the words to the meaning), a sanity of thoughts
and sentiments, the *curiosa felicitas* of his diction, the truth of nature in
the images and descriptions, deep thought and sensibility, and finally the
gift of imagination. Of these virtues or qualities at least three refer to
style; we could, however, argue that all six do so, for how else does the
poet show the gift of imagination except by the kind of language he uses?
Coleridge concludes that this gift is so pre-eminent in Wordworth that it
places him on a level with Shakespeare and Milton as one of the greatest
English poets.

Just as he did when dealing with the defects, Coleridge illustrates each one
of the virtues by one or more examples from Wordsworth's poetry, ranging
over quite a long period, from *Simon Lee* (1798) to *The White Doe* (1815).
Coleridge quotes either some lines or a whole stanza, or sometimes even
several stanzas from this long list of poems. Three whole stanzas are
quoted from *The White Doe* ("the most Coleridgean of Wordsworth's poems"
according to Shawcross), and Coleridge is convinced that all will agree that
it is a perfect example of Wordsworth's best style, having both beauty and
imaginative power. This last and greatest quality is, Coleridge thinks,
exemplified by all the poems listed, but especially by *Yew Trees*, *Resolution
and Independence*, the *Immortality Ode* and *The White Doe*.

Coleridge, of course, does not make such a detailed word-by-word analysis as
some twentieth-century critics like Empson or Cleanth Brooks do, but he
simply names the quality and then illustrates it by one or more examples.
The rest is left to the reader. He may, of course, agree with Coleridge
that the lines or stanzas quoted are good, though he may not necessarily
agree with Coleridge's specific names for or descriptions of the respective
qualities. But this is not really important. What is important is, I think,
the fact that all these qualities refer to the *language of poetry*. It is
therefore logical for Coleridge to assert that "the infallible test of a
blameless style is its *untranslatableness* in words of the same language
without injury to the meaning" (Vol. II, p. 115).

This is one of the two critical aphorisms which Coleridge enounces in ch. I,
namely: "That whatever lines can be translated into other words of the same
language, without diminution of their significance, either in sense, or
association, or in any worthy feeling, are so far vicious in their diction."
The second is "that not the poem which we *read*, but that to which we *return*,
with the greatest pleasure, possesses the genuine power, and claims the name
of *essential poetry*" (Vol. I, p. 14).

The ultimate test of poetry, especially of great poetry, is its untranslatableness, says Coleridge. No better test of what is poetry has yet been
given. And, strange to say, we find here no trace of fancy or imagination.
All we find is a concern with words and their meaning. As Coleridge further

explains, "I include in the *meaning* of a word not only its correspondent object, but likewise all the associations which it recalls. For language is framed to convey not the object alone, but likewise the character, mood and intentions of the person who is representing it" (Vol. II, pp. 115-16). Here Coleridge is clearly anticipating our own preoccupation with the meaning of words, both referential and emotive, and what we call the tone, mood, point of view and persona, which must all be taken into account in a critical analysis of a poem. At all events, the whole passage is surprisingly modern, both in thought and expression.

In ch. XXIII Coleridge analyses in detail the old Spanish play *Atheista Fulminato*, also known by the title of *Don Juan*, the *Libertine*, etc., different versions of which had enjoyed great popularity in Spain and throughout Europe in the seventeenth and eighteenth centuries. (The subject was treated by Gabriel Tellez in Spain (1634), De Villiers (1669) and Molière (1665) in France, Shadwell (1676) in England, Goldoni (1726) in Italy and Grabbe (1829) in Germany, where it was also chosen as the theme of operas by Gluck and Mozart.) Coleridge wants to find the reasons for the popularity of this strange play.

First of all, the play is *imaginative*: neither the characters nor the plot, neither the comic nor the tragic incidents, are real, but are all creatures of the poet's brain. The characters are abstractions and not amenable to the rules of probability. In this they resemble Satan of *Paradise Lost* and Caliban of the *Tempest*. Nevertheless, Don *Juan* is an intelligible character, not because he is a real, but an idealised figure, in the same way as Milton's Satan, the Apollo Belvedere and the Farnese Hercules are. It is what makes the character representative and symbolical, and therefore applicable to whole classes of men.

While not possessing any real probability, the character of Don John (Coleridge is now discussing Shadwell's version of *Don Juan*, the *Libertine*) possesses the only one that matters, i.e. dramatic probability. (In this he is like a number of Shakespearean characters, e.g. Richard, Iago and Edmund.) In order to accept the character and the play in which he occurs, all that is demanded of us is that willing suspension of disbelief which constitutes poetic faith (cf. Vol. I, p. 6). Coleridge illustrates his meaning by quoting a scene from Shadwell's *Libertine*, Act II, and later the concluding scene from Act V and scene iv from Act IV.

Coleridge calls attention to the sublime consistency of Don John's character, remarking on the fine mixture of such desirable qualities as wit, gaiety, generosity, good manners and feelings so that "as our *imagination* sits in judgment", he never seems a ruffian, but remains to the last a highly-bred gentleman. Coleridge concludes that the play has a moral value in showing that such qualities as courage and honour and similar ones are really hollow if regarded as ends in themselves and not as means to a higher end, namely virtue (Vol. II, p. 192).

We are now in a position to sum up Coleridge's criteria of a good play: imagination, intelligibility, characters that are idealised and representative, dramatic probability and, finally, moral value. It is not our concern here to discuss the adequateness of these criteria, only to point out what they are. It should be noted, however, that Coleridge uses the same — or very similar — criteria in his *Shakespearean Criticism*, where he insists again and again on the universality of Shakespeare's characters. For instance, "He said that Shakespeare was almost the only dramatic poet, who by his characters represented a class, and not an individual ...

Shakespeare at one stroke lashed thousands ..." (Raysor, Vol. II, p. 29).

For Coleridge the only good dramatic character is an idealised character, possessing neither the merely individual characteristics of a particular figure nor the generalised ones of an abstraction. The ideal or the idealised character has the living interest of an individual figure as well as the reperesentative or symbolical features of a whole class. In Coleridge's words, "The ideal consists in the happy balance of the generic with the individual" (Vol. II, p. 187). (Be it remarked in passing, that here Coleridge recalls Johnson's view that it is the poet's task to represent the universal, not the particular; or perhaps he means that it is the poet's task to represent the universal in and through the particular.)

I put "imagination" or "imaginativeness" as the first in the list of criteria of a good play. In fact, I should have left it out altogether: for it is not a criterion of greatness at all — it is itself a value term, for which the different qualities serve as criteria. Given these criteria, the play will be called great, good or imaginative; given different criteria, the play will be called mediocre, minor or bad. And this is exactly what Coleridge does in the sequel. For, having analysed *Don Juan* and the *Libertine*, he proceeds to compare and contrast the latter with another play, namely *Bertram* or the *Castle of St. Aldobrand*. This play by Maturin is an adaptation of Shadwell's *Libertine*, and has, according to Coleridge, no dramatic qualities at all, only defects. Coleridge proceeds on as detailed a critical analysis of this play as he did of the *Libertine*. And he convincingly shows its weaknesses which can be summed up in two words: dramatic improbability and immorality. Like other Jacobinical dramas its popularity is due to a confusion and subversion of the natural order of things: instead of giving all the sympathy to the virtuous characters, it gives it to the villains (Vol. II, pp. 192-93). (Coleridge recalls having made the same observation eighteen years ago, in his letters from Germany, i.e. *Satyrane's Letters, III*; cf. *Biographia*, II, 164.)

One last point: Coleridge uses "imaginative" in his analysis of *Don Juan* where we would use "imaginary" or "fictitious"; this is clearly a stretched use of the term (in Coleridge's usual sense), and thus causes confusion. For then, we might well ask, would Coleridge also call a fairy tale, for instance, imaginative? And would he then assign to it the same kind of values as to an imaginative play or poem? At all events, in the case of *Don Juan*, where Coleridge clearly means "imaginary" because "nothing in it belongs to the real world" (cf. a fairy tale), it is difficult to accept his conclusion that the play is, nevertheless, very good and has moral value. Coleridge's whole argument and analysis would have been more convincing had he chosen a different term for describing the play. It is here that his leaning for desynonymisation should have shown itself, which, as he tells us, made him use "fancy" and "imagination" as two distinct terms, which, till his own time, had been used indiscriminately and synonymously.

It should be recalled at this juncture that although Coleridge speaks of the different faculties of the mind in general, and the faculties of the poet in particular — fancy, imagination, memory, judgement and reason — he is not really interested in a psychological or philosophical account of these mental faculties, but in the way they reveal themselves in practice, i.e. in works of literature. In fact, it is in ch. XV, where he describes the poet in ideal perfection, that he shows his great capacity as a practical critic.

The title of the chapter is significant: "The specific symptoms of poetic

power elucidated in a critical analysis of Shakespeare's Venus and Adonis,
and Lucrece." Coleridge's method is as follows: he first lists the four
characteristics of original genius in general, and then he shows how they
are embodied in these two early poems of Shakespeare. The four characteristics are: the sense of musical delight, aloofness, imagination (in its
various forms) and depth and energy of thought. Coleridge shows that these
poetic qualities have their verbal counterparts in the poems, i.e. perfect
sweetness of versification, choice of subjects remote from the private
interests of the poet, the kind of imagery used and mastery of the whole
world of language.

It should be noted that three of the qualities refer to language and only
one to the subject and the poet's relation to it. It is the second quality
which is the most interesting for us, because here Coleridge seems to
anticipate the concept of *impersonality*, detachment or objectivity of the
artist put forward in the twentieth century by T. S. Eliot in "Tradition and
the Individual Talent" (1919) and other essays, and by James Joyce in *A
Portrait of the Artist as a Young Man* (1916). Coleridge describes this
quality as follows: "A second promise of genius is the choice of subjects
very remote from the private interests and circumstances of the writer
himself. At least I have found, that where the subject is taken immediately
from the author's personal sensations and experiences, the excellence of a
particular poem is but an equivocal mark, and often a fallacious pledge, of
genuine poetic power" (Vol. II, pp. 14-15).

Coming from the greatest Romantic critic, such an impersonal conception of
art is surprisingly antiromantic. And its similarity to the views of such
an antiromantic critic as T. S. Eliot is striking. For instance: "It is not
in his personal emotions, the emotions provoked by particular events in his
life, that the poet is in any way remarkable or interesting." On the
contrary, "the more perfect the artist, the more completely separate in him
will be the man who suffers and the mind which creates; the more perfectly
will the mind digest and transmute the passions which are its material".
And again: "Impressions and experiences which are important for the man may
take no place in the poetry, and those which become important in the poetry
may play quite a negligible part in the man, the personality."[10]

Coleridge expresses the same view of the impersonality of the poet in
different words, when he says that in *Venus and Adonis* we feel "the
alienation, and ... the utter *aloofness* of the poet's own feelings, from
those of which he is at once the painter and the analyst...." But what is
even more interesting than this theoretical formulation of the poet's
relation to his work is Coleridge's practical analysis of the poem itself.
The passage is of major importance and is worth quoting in full:

> In the "Venus and Adonis" this proof of poetic power exists even
> to excess. It is throughout as if a superior spirit more
> intuitive, more intimately conscious, even than the characters
> themselves, not only of every outward look and act, but of the
> flux and reflux of the mind in all its subtlest thoughts and
> feelings, were placing the whole before our view; himself mean-
> while unparticipating in the passions, and actuated only by that
> pleasurable excitement which had resulted from the energetic
> fervour of his own spirit in so vividly exhibiting what it had so
> accurately and profoundly contemplated. I think I should have
> conjectured from these poems that even then the great instinct,
> which impelled the poet of the drama, was secretly working in him,
> prompting him by a series and never broken chain of imagery always

vivid and, because unbroken, often minute; by the highest effort of
the picturesque in words, of which words are capable, higher perhaps than was ever realized by any other poet, even Dante not
excepted; to provide a substitute for that visual language, that
constant intervention and running comment by tone, look and
gesture, which in his dramatic works he was entitled to expect from
the players. His Venus and Adonis seem at once the characters
themselves, and the whole representation of those characters by the
most consummate actors. You seem to be told nothing but to see and
hear everything. Hence it is, that from the perpetual activity of
attention required on the part of the reader; from the rapid flow,
the quick change, and the playful nature of the thoughts and
images; and above all from the alienation, and, if I may hazard
such an expression, the utter *aloofness* of the poet's own feelings
from those of which he is at once the painter and analyst; that
though the very subject cannot but detract from the pleasure of a
delicate mind, yet never was poem less dangerous on a moral
account. Instead of doing as Ariosto, and as, still more
offensively, Wieland has done, instead of degrading and deforming
passion into appetite, the trials of love into the struggles of
concupiscence Shakespeare has here represented the animal impulse
itself, so as to preclude all sympathy with it, by dissipating the
reader's notice among the thousand outward images, and now
beautiful, now fanciful circumstances, which form its dresses and
scenery; or by diverting our attention from the main subject by
those frequent witty or profound reflections, which the poet's
ever active mind had deduced from, or connected with, the imagery
and the incidents. The reader is forced into too much action to
sympathize with the merely passive of our nature. As little can a
mind thus roused and awakened be brooded on by mean and indistinct
emotion, as the low, lazy mist can creep upon the surface of a
lake, while a strong gale is driving it onward in waves and
billows (Vol. II, pp. 15-16).

When reading the passage carefully, it will be clearly seen that Coleridge is
trying to express what had not been expressed before, that he is searching
for the right word that will sum up all he wants to say about the right
relation between the artist and the work of art; in short, that he is
searching for the word "impersonality". Such words and phrases as "himself
meanwhile unparticipating in the passions", "You seem to be told nothing, but
to see and hear everything", "the alienation", "the utter *aloofness* of the
poet's own feelings", "to preclude all sympathy with it" (i.e. the animal
impulse represented), all these are like arrows pointing towards the one all-
embracing word — "impersonality". When Coleridge makes such a remark as
"if I may hazard such an expression" before he dares use the following
phrase about "the utter *aloofness* of the poet's own feelings from those of
which he is at once the painter and the analyst", one realises that he is
conscious of treading a new path into an as yet unknown territory. And,
moreover, one realises how great a gulf separates Coleridge from Wordsworth:
one cannot imagine Wordsworth with his view of poetry as "the spontaneous
overflow of powerful feelings" approving of such an impersonality theory of
poetry.

Wordsworth would not, but James Joyce would and does approve. In fact,
Coleridge's passage on *Venus and Adonis* recalls not the *Preface to the
Lyrical Ballads*, but Joyce's passage on the impersonality of the artist in
A Portrait of the Artist as a Young Man: "The personality of the artist, at
first a cry or a cadence or a mood and then a fluid and lambent narrative,

finally refines itself out of existence, impersonalizes itself, so to speak.
The esthetic image in the dramatic form is life purified in and reprojected
from the human imagination. The mystery of esthetic, like that of material
creation, is accomplished. The artist, like the God of creation, remains
within or behind or beyond or above his handiwork, invisible, refined out of
existence, indifferent, paring his fingernails."[11]

Coleridge, as we have seen, was struggling to express the same view; and,
for him, as for Joyce, the artist creating his work could only be compared
to God himself creating the world. In the Gospel according to St. John,
ch. 1, we read: "In the beginning was the Word, and the Word was with God,
and the Word was God." And so it is with the artist, the master of words.
In fact, what Coleridge has so brilliantly shown throughout the *Biographia*,
but specially in ch. XV, is that Shakespeare's imagination and genius is
revealed in the wealth, complexity and mastery of language.

To sum up: the poetic imagination reveals itself, or rather is nothing but,
the poet's ability to handle words, i.e. images, metaphors, similes, figures
of speech; in one word, *language*. Most modern commentators, however, as I
noted earlier, have concentrated on Coleridge's psychological criticism, i.e.
his analysis of the process or processes of composition, in which at times
the poet's "fancy", at others his "imagination", is active; and because this
psychological account of mental faculties and processes represents a
revolutionary change from the earlier neoclassical criticism with its
canons, tenets, principles and rules of composition, Coleridge is hailed as
a great critic, nay as the greatest English critic. But, as I have tried to
show, his greatness does not consist in giving a new psychological account of
the mental faculties, especially the poet's faculties of fancy and imagination, but in his great sensitivity to, and knowledge of, language. This is
seen in all his critical writings — the *Biographia*, the *Shakespearean
Criticism*, the Lectures, the Notes to the Lectures, the Letter on Plagiarism
and such Fragments as "Shakespeare's Poetry" and "Shakespeare's Judgment
Equal to his Genius".

Coleridge's greatness as a critic is expressed most cogently and succinctly
in such statements as "poetry has a logic of its own, as severe as that of
science; and more difficult, because ... dependent on more, and more fugitive
causes" (Vol. I, p. 4), and again, "But if it be asked, by what principles
the poet is to regulate his own style, if he do not adhere closely to the
sort and order of words which he hears in the market, wake, high-road, or
ploughfield? I reply; by principles the ignorance or neglect of which
would convict him of being no *poet*, but a silly or presumptuous usurper of
the name! By the principles of grammar, logic, psychology! In one word by
such knowledge of the facts, material and spiritual, that most pertain to
his art ..." (Vol. II, pp. 63-64).[12]

If Coleridge's words had been heeded, we would not have had to wait for
another hundred and fifty years until criticism finally emerged from its
swaddling clothes and became what it is: an analysis of the various
linguistic devices and complexities by means of which the writer makes his
literary work what it is — itself, and not another thing.[13]

In fine, Coleridge's greatness is not in having coined, defined and analysed
the two main terms of Romantic criticism — fancy and imagination — but in
having shown in his applied criticism that the difference between great and
less great poetry (or poems, parts of poems and plays) is the difference
between an aggregate of words and an organised verbal structure; or between
mere multiplicity and unity-in-variety; in other words, between a mechanical

102   Talmor: The Rhetoric of Criticism

and an organic unity and structure.[14]

A work of art then is a totality, and a unique totality at that. And it is because a work of art is a unique and living totality, just as a living organism, that we cannot remove even the smallest part from it — not even, as Coleridge said of Shakespeare's and Milton's works, a single word — without altering the whole. But this is true only of the really great works of art.[15]

1. S. T. Coleridge, *Biographia Literaria*, ed. J. Shawcross, 2 vols. (London: Oxford University Press, 1st ed. 1907, 1967), p. lxxxv. All references are to this edition and page numbers will appear in the body of the text.
2. For Coleridge poetry is the supreme art. In a fragment entitled "The Permanence of Poetry", he says that his definition of poetry "applies equally to painting and to music as to poetry; and in truth the term 'poetry' is alike applicable to all three. The vehicle alone constitutes the difference ..."; Coleridge, *Shakespearean Criticism*, ed. T. M. Raysor, 2 vols. (London: J. M. Dent and Sons Ltd., Everyman's Library, 1st ed. 1930, 1967), Vol. II, p. 224. All references are to this second edition and page numbers will appear in the body of the text.
3. *On Poetry and Poets* (London: Faber & Faber Ltd., 1957), pp. 115, 116, 117.
4. T. S. Eliot, "Wordsworth and Coleridge", in *The Use of Poetry and the Use of Criticism* (London: Faber & Faber Ltd., 1933, 1964), p. 77.
5. J. Shawcross's view that Coleridge did not really believe in "the so-called 'faculty-psychology'" seems to me unjustified. He argues that this impression was merely created by Coleridge's loose mode of speaking, and that "he did not believe in any such detached activity of the various faculties, as a physiological or psychological fact" (Vol. I, p. lxxxvi). He tries to prove this by quoting one passage from *Table Talk*, July 29, 1830, and another from *The Friend*. But surely this kind of proof is insufficient. For if we suppose that Coleridge said one thing and meant another in all the relevant passages where the terms "faculty" and "faculties" appear (and they are numerous), as well as where the phrases "the faculty of fancy", imagination, reason and understanding appear, this would demand a wholesale rewording of Coleridge's writings into a different terminology, in keeping with the kind of psychology Shawcross thinks better.
6. Edmund Wilson, "Marcel Proust", in *Axel's Castle* (New York: Charles Scribner's Sons, 1931), p. 179.
7. T. S. Eliot, "The Metaphysical Poets", in *Selected Essays* (London: Faber & Faber Ltd., 1932, 1966), p. 286.
8. M. H. Abrams, *The Mirror and the Lamp: Romantic Theory and the Critical Tradition* (New York: W. W. Norton & Co. Inc., 1958).
9. In ch. XII we find the most detailed account of Coleridge's view of the order of the mental faculties. Quoting from an article he contributed to Southey's *Omniana*, he says:

These (the human faculties) I would arrange under the different senses and powers: as the eye, the ear, the touch &c.; the imitative power, voluntary and automatic; the imagination, or shaping and modifying power; the understanding, or the regulative, substantiating and realizing power; the speculative reason, vis theoretica et scientifica, or the power by which we produce or aim

to produce unity, necessity, and universality in all our knowledge
by means of principles a priori; the will, or practical reason;
the faculty of choice (*Germanice*, Willkür) and (distinct both from
the moral will and the choice), the *sensation* of volition, which I
have found reason to include under the head of single and double
touch (Vol. I, pp. 193-194).

10. *Selected Essays*, pp. 18, 20.
11. *The Portable James Joyce*, ed. Harry Levin (New York: The Viking Press,
    1947), pp. 481-482.
12. As we have seen in his numerous references to it, Coleridge was deeply
    interested in logic, and contemplated writing a major work on it, which,
    however, was never completed. Nevertheless, he has left many manu-
    scripts dealing with logical problems. See, for example, Alice D.
    Snyder, *Coleridge on Logic and Learning* (New Haven: Yale University
    Press, 1929) and E. K. Chambers, *Samuel Taylor Coleridge, A Biographical
    Study* (Oxford, 1938).
13. Coleridge's interest in language is so great and, for his time, so
    unique and revolutionary that I. A. Richards, in his book *Coleridge on
    Imagination* (London: Kegan Paul, 1934), rightly calls him "the first
    semasiologist". See also Kathleen Coburn, ed. *Inquiring Spirit* (London:
    Routledge & Kegan Paul Ltd., 1951), chs. III, IV, V, containing
    excerpts from Coleridge's published and unpublished prose writings on
    language, logic, philosophy and literary criticism. Coleridge's
    analytical power and incisiveness is apparent in all the various items,
    but can be seen in the following passage:

> Generally indeed I complain of the German Philosophers (as we are
> most apt to complain of our dearest Friends) — of the Post-
> Kantians at least — for the precipitance with which they pass to
> their own determinations of what the *thing* is, without having
> first enquired what the *word* means when it is used *appropriately*.
> Whenever I convince a man that another term would express his
> meaning far more unexceptionably, the term used was not *appro-
> priate* — but the rule is that the same word should not have
> heterogeneous or even disparate senses. Thus instead of asking,
> *Was Schönheit sey?* [What Beauty is?] I would enquire what *schön*
> properly meant — i.e. what men mean when they use the word *schön*
> in preference to any other epithet (p. 99).

It is difficult to believe that this was written at the beginning of the
nineteenth century and not in our own time, for it immediately recalls
to us Wittgenstein's famous dictum "Don't ask for the meaning, ask for
the use." As Kathleen Coburn observes, Coleridge "was deeply interested
in the philosophical implications of language, and sensitive to problems
of communication. He was aware of the difference between assertive and
emotive power in words, of shades of meaning and the subtleties of
context. He could be casual about grammar in the interests of meaning.
And his own involved hyper-parenthetical style is the vice of these
virtues" (p. 97).
14. A useful supplement to Coleridge's view of the difference between
    mechanical and organic unity and structure may be found in the
    following remarks on Shakespeare's and Beaumont and Fletcher's dramas:

> In respect of style and versification, this play (*The Queen of
> Corinth*) and the following of *Bonduca* may be taken as the best,
> and yet as characteristic, specimens of Beaumont and Fletcher's
> dramas. I particularly instance the first scene of *Bonduca*. Take

Shakespeare's *Richard II*, and having selected some one scene of about the same number of lines, consisting mostly of long speeches, compare it with the first scene in *Bonduca* — not for the idle purpose of finding out which is the better, but in order to see and understand the difference. The latter, that of B. and F., you will find a well-arranged bed of flowers, each having its separate root, and its position determined aforehand by the will of the gardener — each fresh plant a fresh volition. In the former you see an Indian fig-tree, as described by Milton; — all is growth, evolution; — each line, each work, almost, begets the following, and the will of the writer is an interfusion, a continuous agency, and not a series of separate acts. Shakespeare is the height, breadth, and depth of Genius: Beaumont and Fletcher the excellent mechanism, in juxtaposition and succession, of talent. What had a grammatical and logical consistency for the ear — what could be put together and represented to the eye — these poets (Beaumont and Fletcher) took from the ear and the eye, unchecked by any intuition of an inward impossibility; — just as a man might put together a quarter of an orange, a quarter of an apple, and the like of a lemon and a pomegranate and make it look like one round diverse-colored fruit. But nature, which works from within by evolution and assimilation according to a law, can not do so, nor could Shakespeare; for he too worked in the spirit of nature, by evolving the germ from within by the imaginative power according to an idea. For as the power of seeing is to light, so is an idea in mind to a law of nature. They are correlatives, which suppose each other.

(From Coleridge's *Notes and Lectures upon Shakespeare and Some of the Old Poets and Dramatists, with Other Literary Remains, Complete Works*, ed. Shedd, 1871.)

15. See Appendix B, "On Untranslatability" for an analysis of this criterion of the excellence of poems.

Conclusion

At a certain point of history — which, however, it is very difficult, if not impossible, to determine — a new element (or idea, concept, term or word) emerges in the life and language of a people or of several peoples at the same time. In the intellectual, cultural and moral life of Western Europe, this new element, state, quality or value which we have been examining is called Imagination.

Just like such terms as "sincerity", "authenticity", or "alienation" in our own time, imagination is really an umbrella term with many different meanings or connotations: individuality, originality, subjectivity, sincerity, the true self and free creativity. Imagination and its many cognates (image, to image, to imagine, imaginativeness, imaginary, creative or poetic imagination, freedom of imagination) are generally associated with that period of intellectual and cultural history we call the Romantic period, extending roughly from the end of the eighteenth century to the end of the nineteenth and early twentieth century. What Reason was to the Neoclassics, Imagination was to the Romantics, a single concept which contained in itself a whole view of life and of man.

We must remember, however, that these two words were in current use not only among writers, poets and critics we call the Neoclassics and the Romantics, but were to be found in all spheres of human activity — religious, moral, social, political and cultural. In short, certain terms at certain times are all-pervasive, and take on for later periods the status of symbols of that time. Say "neoclassic" to anyone and that person will immediately think: "Oh yes, Reason, Nature, and that lot." Say "romantic" and he will think: "Oh yes, Imagination, fancy, feeling, spontaneous outpourings, love of nature, and all that."

But neither of these reactions do justice to or really encompass the all-pervasiveness, complexity, ambiguity and ambivalence of these and similar terms. To take but one example, such a word as Nature has a completely different meaning for the eighteenth or the nineteenth century, i.e. for the Neoclassics and the Romantics: whereas for the former it always and only means human nature — that is essential, universal and changeless human nature, the same always and everywhere — for the latter it means, above all,

physical nature and its phenomena — mountains, sea, storms, sunsets,
fields, trees, flowers.

If the Romantics and we ourselves are talking about human nature, then we
generally mean the nature of man as an individual, i.e. those personal
traits and qualities that are distinctive and which make each man unique.
Both these views — of the sameness and the uniqueness of man — find
support in the works of literature and art of different ages and cultures.
For the Neoclassics, as we have seen, for a Hume and a Johnson for example,
those works of art are great which have stood the test of time; and they
have stood the test of time *because* they embody and express *quod semper,
quod ubique*. For the Romantics, on the other hand, those works are great
that embody and express the poet's imagination, that unique state, quality
or value which is his own and not another's. For Coleridge, for instance,
Shakespeare's greatness is his imaginative or creative power, his capacity
to imagine and create the most varied dramatic characters. At the same
time, as we have noted, Coleridge foreshadows the modern view of the
impersonality of the artist, who presents his characters without telling us
what he thinks about them and what we should think and feel about them. The
great artist allows us to use our own imagination in our aesthetic
experience and evaluation of his work. We see here the origin of those
important modern critical concepts — "telling" and "showing" — which have
become so widely used in the second half of the twentieth century.

Like "sincerity" and "authenticity", imagination is also a battlecry of
radical thinkers, poets and critics who, by means of it, declare their
intention to strike out on new untried paths of discovery, creation and
expression. The changes which certain words announce and signify, the
changes in ways of thinking, feeling and expression, are sometimes sudden,
but sometimes come about only very gradually, taking a long time to emerge,
to be recognised and accepted. Very often, especially in periods of
transition, when the old modes of conduct, thinking, feeling and expression
are still well established, but the new ways are beginning to be voiced and
noticed, they are often received with irony and are naturally resisted and
criticised. We find this happening at the end of the eighteenth century,
at the time when the *Lyrical Ballads* were published, announcing a new way of
writing poetry and a new poetic and critical credo. The way for Romanticism
had been prepared for a long time; we find already in the second half of the
eighteenth century certain new words signifying change such as "sentiment",
"feeling", "sensibility", "uncertainty". But then, at a definite moment,
Romanticism suddenly came into being: it was there, for all to see. And it
took them all by surprise. Wordsworth told his contemporaries that he was
"a man speaking to men". Coleridge in his literary autobiography talked
about such unheard-of things as the primary and secondary imagination,
fancy, organic unity, the right and wrong way of writing poems, true and
false criticism and critics. And both Wordsworth and Coleridge were writing
their poems, critical essays and books as if the established poets and
critics with their rules, canons, principles and tenets did not exist or did
not count. Of course they were attacked and criticised; of course neoclassical authorities rose up to defend their rights, their literary and social
status, but it was already too late: a new period had begun.

Imagination is also a polemical concept. For the new Romantic poets,
writers and critics of the eighteenth and nineteenth century it expressed
all those things they hold dear — freedom, creativity, selfhood, independence — as against those things they condemn — received opinion, "poetic
diction", mechanical criticism, mechanical philosophy, the imitation of past
models and blind obedience to prescriptive criticism. And yet they too

accepted an authority: but it was not an outer, established or institutionalised authority; it was their own, the authority of their own conscience,
whether artistic or moral. They never gave a name to it, but Eliot has
called it — derogatively — the "Inner Voice". It is the voice of a man's
or a poet's own self, his individuality, his conscience.

The difference between the seventeenth and eighteenth centuries and the
nineteenth and twentieth centuries is not only a difference in ways of life
and conduct, but a difference of language and rhetoric. In the literary
and critical idiom we describe the difference in terms of Neoclassicism and
Romanticism. I have examined the language or rhetoric of neoclassical and
romantic critics and have emphasised — against most modern commentators —
that the difference is not describable in psychological terms, but only in
linguistic or rhetorical ones. In sum, the difference between neoclassical
poets and critics and romantic poets and critics is not a difference of
psychological and philosophical theories and doctrines, but a difference of
language and rhetoric.

Davenant, Hobbes and Dryden

Davenant's *Preface to Gondibert* and Hobbes's *Answer to Davenant* were published together in Paris in 1650 and were reprinted one year later in London, together with Davenant's unfinished epic. Modern critics generally agree about the minor value of the poem, and would generally subscribe to the view of E. M. W. Tillyard in his exhaustive study *The English Epic and its Background* that "As a poem *Gondibert* has no essential claim to be an epic, nor has it an important place in the history of the epic form."

According to Tillyard, the Preface is by far more important than the epic *Gondibert* and "is one of the landmarks of seventeenth-century criticism and contains the earliest English statement of certain epic neo-classical doctrines". Although the epic "is indeed far from what parts of its preface would suggest", it has at least an historical importance, namely "that it prompted Dryden to use its metre for *Annus Mirabilis*".[1]

However, even if Dryden's poem is greater than Davenant's, present-day readers read neither the one nor the other. Epic poetry and heroic plays may have been the most important literary genre in the seventeenth century, but even then they soon went out of fashion, to be replaced by other genres — political satires, bourgeois comedies, sentimental novels and poems. Dryden himself, who wrote five heroic plays, is chiefly remembered for his verse satires — *The Medal, MacFlecknoe* and *Absalom and Achitophel* — rather than for his epic poems or heroic plays. It is worth remarking in this connection that Dryden himself freely acknowledged his debt to and admiration for Davenant in many of his critical prefaces. It seems strange, therefore, that modern critics, while repeating again and again Dryden's great debt to Hobbes in his theory of imagination and poetic composition, hardly ever mention his debt to Davenant.

It is enough to look at Dryden's prefaces and read what *he* has to say about Davenant and Hobbes to see that the truth is quite different. Thus Dryden not only gratefully acknowledges his debt to Davenant for his alternately rhymed stanza, but also regards him as an able critic. In his "Preface to *Annus Mirabilis*" (1666) he writes that "I have dwelt too long upon the choice of my stanza, which you may remember is much better defended in the preface to *Gondibert*."[2] And as early as the "Epistle Dedicatory of *The Rival Ladies*"

(1664), which is his first critical essay, Dryden, defending the use of rhyme as superior to blank verse, remarks that "we are acknowledging for the noblest use of it to Sir William D'Avenant, who at once brought it upon the stage, and made it perfect, in the *Siege of Rhodes*" (Vol. I, p. 7).

But it is in the "Prefatory Essay to *The Conquest of Granada*" (1672), whose subject is *Heroic Plays*, that Dryden naturally recalls Davenant's epic and his Preface at length. He praises Davenant for "that excellent groundwork which he laid" for the practitioners of heroic plays who followed him, remarking that "since it is an easy thing to add to what already is invented, we ought all of us, without envy to him, or partiality to ourselves, to yield him the precedence in it" (Vol. I, p. 150). And then Dryden gives a short but fairly full account of Davenant's view of what a heroic poem is, or rather ought to be: *"That it ought to be dressed in a more familiar and easy shape; more fitted to the common actions and passions of human life; and, in short, more like a glass of Nature, showing us ourselves in our ordinary habits, and figuring a more practicable virtue to us, than was done by the Ancients or Moderns.* Thus he takes the image of an heroic poem from the drama, or stage poetry; and accordingly intended to divide it into five books, representing the same number of acts; and every book into several cantos, imitating the scenes which compose our acts" (Vol. I, p. 151).

Here Dryden gives us in a single passage, in his clear modern prose, the gist of Davenant's long, ornate and wordy Preface. We should note that Dryden fully agrees with Davenant that heroic poetry is the highest literary genre and that its function is to be "like a glass of Nature", i.e. a true representation of human passions, character and actions.

We have noted that Dryden refers to Davenant in a number of critical essays and that he freely acknowledges his debt to him as poet and dramatist. Let us now see what place and importance Dryden assigns to Hobbes in his critical essays.

There are only three references to Hobbes altogether. The first occurs in the "Preface to *Sylvae*" (1685), where Dryden says that he knew of no one so like Lucretius "as our poet and philosopher of Malmesbury" (Vol. I, p. 259). Nevertheless, there is a difference between them: Lucretius, "who, though often in the wrong, yet seems to deal *bonâ fide* with his reader, and tells him nothing but what he thinks; in which plain sincerity, I believe, he differs from our Hobbes, who could not but be convinced, or at least doubt, of some eternal truths which he had opposed" (ibid.). Whereas the first statement expresses frank admiration for Hobbes's "magisterial authority" and confidence in his own reason, in which he is like Lucretius, the second qualifies this admiration considerably for moral reasons — insincerity.

The only other essay in which Hobbes is mentioned is the "Preface to the *Fables*", Dryden's last critical essay. He remarks that "In the mean time to follow the third of my discourse (as thoughts, according to Hobbes, have always some connexion), so from Chaucer I was led to think of Boccace, who was not only his contemporary, but also pursued the same studies ..." (Vol. II, p. 248). The longest passage refers to Hobbes's translation of Homer: "Mr. Hobbes, in his translation of the *Ilias* (studying poetry as he did mathematics too late), Mr. Hobbes, I say, begins the praise of Homer where he should have ended it" (Vol. II, p. 252), i.e. with his diction.

Here Dryden clearly shows his disapproval of Hobbes: not only is his translation "bald", but what is far more important is Dryden's disagreement regarding the relative importance of diction, design, disposition, manners and thoughts in an epic poem. Whereas for Hobbes "the first beauty of an epic poem consists in diction; that is, in the choice of words, and harmony of numbers", for Dryden "the words are the colouring of the work, which, in the order of nature, is last to be considered" (ibid.).

From the passages quoted we see that Dryden's attitude to Hobbes and Davenant is fundamentally different: whereas he has only praise and admiration for Davenant, he shows disapproval, disagreement with and reservations for Hobbes. The generally accepted view of modern critics, that Dryden made considerable use of Hobbes's ideas and views on philosophy, psychology, ethics, politics and poetry, seems to me mistaken and unsupported by sufficient evidence.

REFERENCES

1. E. M. W. Tillyard, *The English Epic and its Background* (New York: Oxford University Press, 1966; 1st ed. 1954), p. 428.
2. *Essays of John Dryden*, ed. W. P. Ker (New York: Russell & Russell, 1961; 1st ed. 1899), 2 vols. Vol. I, p. 12. All subsequent references are to this edition and are given in the body of the text.

APPENDIX B

On Untranslatability

We saw in the last chapter that Coleridge regarded the work of art as a unique totality, a living organism, from which no part (not even the smallest) could be removed without altering the whole. Let us now examine this view in detail and consider how it may be linked to the concept of organic unity as a valid criterion of poetic excellence.

I

In ch. I of the *Biographia Literaria*, Coleridge gives us what he considers the two most general criteria of the best poetic style: "As the result of all my reading and meditation, I abstracted two critical aphorisms, deeming them to comprise the conditions and criteria of poetic style; first that not the poem which we have *read*, but that to which we *return*, with the greatest pleasure, possesses the genuine power, and claims the name of *essential poetry*. Second, that whatever lines can be translated into other words of the same language, without diminution of their significance, either in sense, or association, or in any worthy feeling, are so far vicious in their diction."[1] And a little later he adds that "I was wont boldly to affirm, that it would be scarcely more difficult to push a stone out from the pyramids with the bare hand, than to alter a word, or the position of a word, in Milton or Shakespeare, (in their most important works at least,) without making the author say something else, or something worse, than he does say" (Vol. I, p. 15).

What Coleridge calls "essential poetry" is true or real poetry, i.e. poetry that possesses what he regards as the defining characteristics of poetry, and which distinguish it from science on the one hand and all other literary genres on the other. Let us call this first criterion of poetry "plenitude".[2] Coleridge, however, does not give it a name and does not return to it again. In his note on the line "not the poem which we have read etc.", Shawcross comments that "the facts of our returning to it proves that its attraction did not lie in the novelty of the matter" (Vol. I, p. 209). It seems to me that Coleridge meant more than just this. For, if Shawcross were right, it would follow that we might return to the poem once or twice but not more, since by the second or third time the "matter" of the poem would already be familiar to us and hence no longer surprising. I take it, therefore, that Coleridge had in mind something more inclusive than that: I suggest he meant what I call plenitude. True or real or essential poems are those that have plenitude, that are multilayered and multivalent, i.e. that possess values and meanings that are not immediately apparent and are therefore not fully exhausted even by many readings. Some old English ballads, some anonymous medieval lyrics, some Elizabethan sonnets and many of Shakespeare's songs possess this quality of many-layeredness and plenitude which makes them inexhaustible after many readings, and hence always new. However, since Coleridge does not enlarge on this criterion any further, it is not our concern here.

It is the second criterion which Coleridge later calls *untranslatableness* (and which I call Untranslatability) that is his basic and most inclusive criterion of poetic value. In ch. XXII, his longest and most detailed chapter of practical criticism, where he analyses the characteristic defects and beauties of Wordsworth's poetry, Coleridge writes:

> In poetry, in which every line, every phrase, may pass the ordeal of deliberation and deliberate choice, it is possible, and barely possible, to attain that ultimatum which I have ventured to propose as the infallible test of a blameless style; its *untranslatableness* in words of the same language without injury to the meaning. Be it observed, however, that I include in the *meaning* of a word not only its correspondent object, but likewise all the associations which it recalls. For language is framed to convey not the object alone, but likewise the character, mood and intentions of the person who is representing it" (Vol. II, pp. 115-116).

This passage, together with the one from ch. I quoted above, are the main passages to whose explication and interpretation we now turn.

The infallible test of a blameless style, i.e. of the best style of poetry, is, says Coleridge, its untranslatability. If his sentence stopped here there would be no difficulty in interpreting it; for we could say that Coleridge simply holds that poetry, which is man's highest and most concentrated form of utterance, whether in speech or writing, is so bound up with the language in which it is uttered that much of its meaning would simply be lost were we to translate it into another language. Different natural languages have different sound patterns, rhythms, metaphors, puns; they have different grammatical and syntactical structures; therefore much of the meaning and music of the original work would be lost in translation. And what is lost is that "general atmospheric suggestiveness of poetic language — the aura of meanings which words cannot help having round them — which, however, they have not through any natural resemblance to things, but through resemblance to other words" of the same language. As W. K. Wimsatt, in his essay on "Verbal Style: Logical and Counterlogical", says, "If the *sun* is an appropriate symbol of a *son*, then that is true in France as well as in England. But in France Herbert's poem ["The Sonne"] could not be written, because they have not *sun* and *son* but *fils* and *soleil*. Similarly, if the rain is something like human tears, that is true in England as well as in France. But certain poems could be written in French and not in English, because we have *weep* and *rain*, they have *pleurer* and *pleuvoir*. ('Il pleure dans mon coeur Comme il pleut sur la ville.')"[3]

If certain poems can or cannot be written in English or in French, then analogously certain poems can or cannot be translated into French or into English. At this point we touch on the problem of translation and hence of translatability.

TRANSLATABILITY

It is worth recalling that Coleridge himself discusses the possibility and
the difficulties of translating poetry on several occasions. Thus, for
instance, in his *Shakespearean Criticism*, after enumerating the special
characteristics of the main European languages, he illustrates the difficulty
of translating an English poem into German by quoting a stanza from one of
Gray's poems, the *Stanzas to Bentley*. After remarking on the specific
advantages of German, French, Italian and Greek which "contains all the
excellences of all languages", Coleridge enlarges on the characteristics of
the English language:

> But in English I find that which is possessed by no other modern
> language, and which, as it were, appropriates it to the drama. It
> is a language made out of many, and it has consequently many words,
> which originally had the same meaning; but in the progress of
> society those words have gradually assumed different shades of
> meaning. Take any homogenous language, such as German, and try to
> translate into it the following lines:-
>
>   'But not to one, in this benighted age,
>   Is that diviner inspiration given,
>   That burns in Shakespeare's or in Milton's page,
>   The pomp and prodigality of heaven.'
>
>   Gray's *Stanzas to Bentley*.
>
> In German it would be necessary to say 'the pomp and *spendthrift-
> ness* of heaven, 'because the German has not, as we have, one word
> with two such distinct meanings, one expressing the nobler, the
> other the baser idea of the same action.[4]

The German word Coleridge probably has in mind is *Verschwendung*, which, as he
rightly remarks, has a negative meaning. "Prodigality" and *Verschwendung*
have therefore a quite different suggestiveness, aura of meanings and
implications.

In ch. XVI of the *Biographia* Coleridge again deals with the same problem in
his comparison of the poetry of the fifteenth and sixteenth centuries with
that of his own time. In a long footnote he praises the Madrigals of
Giovambatista Strozzi, published in Florence in 1593. He finds them perfect
because they possess "that complete adequateness of the matter to the manner"
as well as tenderness and delicacy. And then he adds the following telling
observation: "After what I have advanced, it would appear presumption to
offer a translation; even if the attempt were not discouraged by the different genius of the English mind and language, which demands a denser body of
thought as the condition of a high polish, than the Italian" (Vol. II, p. 25).
And so Coleridge does not translate the Madrigals but simply transcribes
nine of them in Italian.

It is obvious that Coleridge is fully aware of the difficulties involved in
translating poetry from one language into another, no matter what the original
language is. He makes it clear that any translation, even the best, cannot be
equal to the original, due to the different characters of different languages. As in the instance cited above, he prefers not to attempt a translation

so as not to diminish the completeness or perfection of the original poems.

We can conclude from the foregoing passages that for Coleridge every translation, even the best, is incapable of doing justice to the original: no
adequate and complete rendering in a different language is possible, the
reason being that by its very nature poetry in general and the highest
poetry in particular has "a perfect appropriateness of words to the meaning"
(Vol. II, p. 115). And since you cannot separate words from their meaning,
it is only *these* words, in *this* order, in *this* language, which really
convey *the* meaning the poet intended. In one word, translation is but a
poor substitute for the original literary work.

In our time such a view has the support of two great modern philosophers of
language and logicians, namely Frege and Quine. Frege writes that "The more
exactly scientific an exposition is the less will the nationality of its
author be discernible and the easier will it be to translate. On the other
hand, the constituents of language to which I want to call attention here,
make the translation of poetry very difficult, even make a complete
translation almost always impossible, for it is in precisely that in which
poetic value largely consists that languages differ most."[5]

This view is shared by Quine. In "Two Dogmas of Empiricism", where he
examines the notion of synonymy of two linguistic forms, he is careful to
point out that he is "not concerned here with synonymy in the sense of
complete identity in psychological associations or poetic quality; indeed no
two expressions are synonymous in such a sense".[6]

In other words, in a poetic context no words, phrases or expressions are
interchangeable or translatable by others without incurring a change or loss
of meaning: in short, in poetry no two words or expressions can be regarded
as completely synonymous or identical.

II

Having considered, though only very briefly, what Coleridge thinks of
translation and hence of translatability, let us now return to the more
important, though related, concept of "untranslatability". As we have seen,
Coleridge holds that it is impossible to translate poetry (i.e. all literature) from one language into another; but he also holds the more extreme
view that it is impossible to translate lines of poetry "into other words of
the *same* language, without diminution of their significance, either in sense,
or association, or in any worthy feeling" (Vol. I, p. 14). Let us
examine the meaning and implications of this statement for Coleridge's
theory of poetry.

In this passage Coleridge has introduced into English criticism a concept of
great importance, a concept whose far-reaching implications have not yet
been generally recognised. For what the concept of untranslatability
implies is: that the meaning of a word, phrase, line, stanza and finally of
a whole poem *is* the words used. Only these words, in this order, are the
meaning of the poem. To use a modern term, we could say that untranslatability is a basic concept for a semantic definition of poetry.

While proposing untranslatability as the test or criterion of poetic
excellence, Coleridge does not think that this is a test which is
universally, or even generally, applicable. Himself a poet and critic, he
knows of course that there are a great number of poems — possibly a
majority of poems — where this test is inapplicable. It is those poems

where a translation into other words of the same language is possible that
are not the best, or, in Coleridge's words, "they are so far vicious in
their diction" (Vol. I, p. 15). We could render this by means of a
syllogism:

"If the words are translatable into others, without loss of meaning, the
poem is bad. These words are translatable. Therefore this poem is bad."
And conversely, "If the words are untranslatable, the poem is good. These
words are untranslatable. Therefore this poem is good." Coleridge
reinforces his principle of untranslatability by citing Milton and Shakespeare as a test case: he claims that it would be impossible "to alter a
word, or the position of a word, in Milton or Shakespeare (in their most
important works at least) without making the author say something else, or
something worse, than he does say" (Vol. I, p. 15). For him, this clinches
and concludes the whole argument.

SYNONYMY

In all his critical writings Coleridge shows his continual preoccupation
with words and their meanings. His various dicta on Untranslatability, the
problems of translation and the nature and language of poetry are problems
that greatly preoccupy many modern philosophers. We can call them the
problems of the philosophy of language, e.g. meaning, identity, reference,
equivalence, synonymity or synonymy of words and expressions.

Let us take some simple examples of synonymy: bachelor — unmarried man;
acorn — nut fruit; father — male parent; Morning Star — Evening Star;
Elizabeth II — the present Queen of England.

Now this kind of synonymy of two words or expressions consists in their
interchangeability without change in truth value. This definition of
synonymy or sameness of meaning reduces the baffling problem of meaning to
a semantic problem of words or wordhood. However, in poetry something more
is involved, i.e. not only the bare cognitive meaning of a word or an
expression (variously called its reference, denotation, lexical content or
extensionality), but more importantly its poetic synonymy (variously called
its range of connotations, associations, emotive import or suggestions).[7]
Coleridge, as we have seen, believes that in a poem, especially a good poem,
no word is translatable into another, i.e. that there are no two words or
expressions that are completely identical, interchangeable or synonymous.

Let us try and illustrate Coleridge's principle of untranslatability by some
concrete examples, i.e. let us see what happens if we replace or change a
single word in a line of poetry. In *Richard III*, shortly before he is
killed in battle, the King cries: "A horse! a horse! my kingdom for a horse"
(V. iv. 7). And thus, as Clemen puts it, "With his famous cry — perhaps
the best-known line from Shakespeare's early Histories — Richard offers
everything he has achieved with so much effort and spilt blood in exchange
for a horse. At the end, fighting desperately for his bare life, the great
gambler stakes all he has upon this final cast."[8]

Now let us replace "horse" by some other word: gelding, stallion, nag or
steed. According to the *Webster Dictionary* all these words are synonymous.
(The dictionary lists under "horse" — gelding or stallion; under "nag" it
puts "sometimes any horse"; "steed" — "riding-horse, literary term".) So
we're on safe ground. Now when we replace the common word "horse" by any
other synonym, e.g. gelding, stallion, nag or steed, we get a sentence with

the same *cognitive meaning*, but with a quite different *poetic meaning* (or connotations, associations, import or suggestions). "A steed! a steed! my kingdom for a steed!" How does it sound? It does not sound right, I think. Why? Well, this is the question for which Coleridge's untranslatability is the only answer.

My second example is of a different type, involving not synonyms but homonyms or homophones. In Thomas Nashe's poem *Summer's Last Will and Testament* (also called *In Plague Time*) we have the following stanza:

> Beauty is but a flower
> Which wrinkles will devour;
> Brightness falls from the air,
> Queens have died young and fair,
> Dust hath closed Helen's eye,
> I am sick, I must die.
> Lord, have mercy on us!

The line "Brightness falls from the air" is the one that concerns us here. Until recently no other version was known and the line presented no special problems for critics of poetry. But as soon as the suggestion was made that Nashe wrote and meant not "air" but "hair", a number of critical problems arose. What are the implications if Nashe really wrote and meant "hair" and not "air" as was generally believed? In what sense can we say that there is a fundamental difference between the two words, and hence between the two lines and finally in the whole poem? There are of course different answers according to the different views and interpretations of different critics. Thus William Empson, for instance, argues that if Nashe really wrote or meant "hair" then, "though less imaginative, this is very adequate; oddly enough (it is electricity and the mysterious vitality of youth which have *fallen* from the *hair*) carries much the same suggestion as the other version; and gives the relief of a single direct meaning. Elizabethan pronounciation was very little troubled by snobbery, and it is conceivable that Nashe meant both words to take effect in some way."[9]

As we see, Empson's way out of the difficulty is quite easy: first, he claims that even if we replace the one word "air" by the quite different word "hair" (a homonym for the Elizabethans but not for us and a synonym for neither), the meaning of the line (and hence of the poem) is unaffected, since the two words nevertheless carry the same suggestions (or associations, or connotations or what have you). Moreover, in keeping with his theory that ambiguity itself is one of the distinguishing marks of poetry, especially of great poetry, he suggests that Nashe consciously wished the word to be ambiguous, and hence we are not forced to choose between the two versions: we can have both.

We can only surmise what Coleridge would have said to this refusal to choose between alternative possibilities: but, judging from his definite views regarding untranslatability, he would, I think, definitely reject such an approach. For Coleridge there is a fundamental difference between what is right and what is wrong, or only approximately right, in poetry. In the best poetry there is, Coleridge says again and again, "an austere purity of language both grammatically and logically; in short a perfect appropriateness of the words to the meaning" (Vol. II, p. 115). And, as we have seen, he firmly believed that no two words, phrases, expressions or figures of speech can be equally appropriate: different words *mean* different things in a poetic context.

My last example comes from Yeats's poem *Among School Children*. It is in
stanza VI and reads:

> Plato thought nature but a spume that plays
> Upon a ghostly paradigm of things;
> Soldier Aristotle played the taws
> Upon the bottom of a king of kings;

We know that this is not what Yeats wrote and intended: a printer's error
had changed the original "solider" to "soldier" and this has remained the
accepted version. Like Nashe's "air/hair", Yeats's "solider/soldier" has
become one of the critical puzzles that preoccupy literary critics: which
version is the true one? Which shall we choose? The original one of Nashe
and Yeats or the generally known and accepted version which Nashe and Yeats
did not write? Some critics favour the one, some the other, supporting
their respective views with a whole battery of critical arguments. To take
but one example, A. J. Ellis in his article "Intention and Interpretation in
Literature" argues that "we should insist on the restoration of the lines as
Yeats wrote them", especially because "we wish to have a standard text and
how can we achieve that except by printing what the poet wrote?"[10]

Another critic holds the opposite view. Thus the American critic Delmore
Schwartz has advanced "his well-known interpretation to the effect that the
expression 'soldier Aristotle' alludes to a legend that Aristotle accompanied
Alexander on his military expedition to India. Since there is obviously a
contrast intended between the unworldliness of Plato and the down-to-earth-
ness of Aristotle, Schwartz' military interpretation accords well with the
rest of the poem."[11] However, just like A. J. Ellis, Dr. F. Cioffi also
rejects this view, claiming that "now that we know the error, wouldn't we
insist on the restoration of the lines as Yeats wrote them and regard the
view that there is a military allusion in the line as a mistake?"[12]

One possible way out of the difficulty could be that of Beardsley who makes
a distinction between what words mean and what people mean. And so we come
back again to the question of the meaning of words, expressions and
sentences. It follows that one can give an account of "the meaning of a
sentence" or "the meaning of a poem" in terms of words and their "public
conventions of usage". As Beardsley has put it, "For what the sentence
means depends not on the whim of the individual, and his mental vagaries,
but upon public conventions of usage that are tied up with habit patterns in
the whole speaking community."[13]

Similarly, "the meaning of a poem" can also be discovered in the same way,
i.e. "it is discovered through the semantics and syntax of a poem, through
our habitual knowledge of the language, through grammars, dictionaries, and
all the literature which is the source of dictionaries, in general through
all that makes a language and culture".[14]

It seems to me that such a verbal or semantic formulation of "the meaning of
a poem" would have been approved by Coleridge. In all the passages quoted
earlier we noted the great importance he gives to the logical and grammatical
structure of language; we also noted that for Coleridge the best poet is he
whose poetry exhibits this logical and grammatical structure, what he calls
"a perfect appropriateness of the words to the meaning" (Vol. II, p. 115).
Furthermore, as he tells us in ch. I, for him "no authority could avail in
opposition to Truth, Nature, Logic, and the Laws of Universal Grammar"
(Vol. I, p. 14); and, in the same chapter, he recalls with admiration his
stern teacher, the Rev. James Bowyer, who taught him "that Poetry, even that

of the loftiest and, seemingly, that of the wildest odes, had a logic of its own, as severe as that of science; and more difficult, because more subtle, more complex, and dependent on more, and more fugitive causes. In the truly great poets, he would say, there is a reason assignable not only for every word, but for the position of every word; and I well remember that, availing himself of the synonimes to the Homer of Didymus, he made us attempt to show, with regard to each, *why* it would not have answered the same purpose; and *wherein* consisted the peculiar fitness of the word in the original text" (Vol. I, pp. 4-5).

Coleridge's whole approach to the question of the language of poetry and the meaning of a poem is linguistic or semantic. In his analyses and textual explications of various poems and plays, Coleridge does not ask what the poet means, but he asks what the *poem* means (though, as Beardsley points out, "since a poem, in a sense, is what it means, to discover what the *poem* means is to discover what the *poet* meant").[15] In his objective analyses of poems and plays — partial though these analyses may be — Coleridge tries to show that the logical and grammatical structure underlying poems, especially good poems, can be made explicit.

It logically follows that there *are* valid "principles of writing", principles that both the poet and the critic have to know. As Coleridge says, "The ultimate end of criticism is much more to establish the principles of writing, than to furnish *rules* how to pass judgment on what has been written by others; if indeed it were possible that the two could be separated" (Vol. II, p. 63). Furthermore, "if it be asked, by what principles the poet is to regulate his own style, ... I reply; by principles, the ignorance or neglect of which would convict him of being no *poet*, but a silly or presumptuous usurper of the name! By the principles of grammar, logic, psychology! In one word by such a knowledge of the facts, material and spiritual, that most appertain to his art, ... " (Vol. II, pp. 63-64).

To round off the present topic, we shall now consider Coleridge's other criterion of poetic excellence, namely organic unity.

III

ORGANIC UNITY

In ch. XIV of the *Biographia*, Coleridge gives us his famous definition of a poem: "A poem is that species of composition, which is opposed to works of science, by proposing for its *immediate* object pleasure, not truth; and from all other species (having *this* object in common with it) it is discriminated by proposing to itself such delight from the *whole*, as is compatible with a distinct gratification from each component part" (Vol. II, p. 10).

It is not our concern here to examine Coleridge's distinction between poetry and science regarding their special "object", end or purpose. It should be noted, however, that for Coleridge poetry means not only literature but all art: "All the fine arts are different species of poetry", he writes in one of his Aesthetical Essays ("On the Principles of Genial Criticism", (Vol. II, p. 220). And after dividing the fine arts into poetry of language, poetry of the ear or music, poetry of the eye or sculpture and graphic poetry or painting, Coleridge again distinguishes poetry from science in terms of their different end, object or purpose, i.e. pleasure and truth. Does this mean that the sciences cannot give pleasure or that poetry cannot express truths? Of course not. As Coleridge remarks, "The sciences indeed may and will give a high and pure pleasure; and the Fine Arts may lead to

important truth, and be in various ways useful in the ordinary meaning of
the word; but these are not the direct and characteristic ends, and we
define things by their peculiar, not their common properties" (Vol. II,
p. 221).

Poetry then gives pleasure; and the pleasure is derived from the poem as a
whole, as well as, or rather because of, the pleasure derived from its
component parts. This is perfectly in keeping with Coleridge's definition
of poetry in terms of words and their meaning which could be called a
semantic definition of poetry. We can now understand why Coleridge sets
such high value on the untranslatability of any word into another of the
same language: we can neither change a word, nor the position of a word in a
line of poetry without changing the meaning of the line and possibly of the
whole poem. Coleridge's view of the organic unity of the poem is a general-
isation of his view of the value of every single word and of the whole word
order in a poem. Or, alternately, we could say that, given his view of
organic unity as the defining characteristic of poetry, he deduces from it
the importance and value of its constitutive parts, i.e. stanzas, lines,
phrases and finally single words. In Coleridge's words, "The spirit of
poetry, like all other living powers ... must embody in order to reveal
itself; but a living body is of necessity an organized one — and what is
organization, but the connection of parts to a whole, so that each part is
at once end and means!"[16]

Coleridge's principle of organic unity is related to his general definition
of beauty as "The Reduction of Many to One" or simply "Multëity in Unity"
(Vol. II, pp. 238, 232). This definition of beauty as multiplicity in unity
applies also to art or poetry: "It is the figured language of thought, and
is distinguished from nature by the unity of all the parts in one thought or
idea." And Coleridge concludes that "a work of art will be just in proportion as it adequately conveys the thought, and rich in proportion to the
variety of parts which it holds in unity" (Vol. II, p. 255).

In sum, the best work of art is that which embodies the greatest variety of
elements in a unified whole: its unity is like that of a living organism in
which all the parts are inter-related, interdependent and harmoniously
integrated into one unified whole.

We have now reached the point where we can attempt to answer the question:
Do we accept Coleridge's untranslatability as a criterion of poetic
excellence? We should recall, however, that Coleridge himself was fully
aware that his criterion is only an ideal which only the very greatest poets,
only in their very greatest poems, ever attain. The criterion is an ideal
limit, marking the ultimum of perfection for which every poet strives, but
only very few fully attain. It follows that it is not a criterion that is
or can be widely and generally applicable. In Coleridge's criticism,
however, it is part of his general Kantian Idealist aesthetics. Thus, the
view of the work of art as a living organism, where all the parts are
related as are the parts of a growing plant or of a living body, is fully in
harmony with the principle of untranslatability: just as you cannot cut off
any part of a plant or body without mutilating it, so you cannot change a
word or the position of a word without changing the whole. But if no
change or mutilation is apparent, then, according to Coleridge, that poem
is not really a living whole and has no organic unity. The statue of the
Venus de Milo is a case in point: no sculptor has dared replace her missing
arms and hands.

In conclusion: Coleridge's principle of untranslatability is a valid

principle of poetic excellence. It derives from a semantic definition of
poetry, and it assumes that there is only one right meaning for a word,
phrase or line within a poetic context. And as such it is logically
connected to Coleridge's definition of a work of art as multiplicity-in-
unity or many-in-one, where the best work is that which holds the greatest
variety of parts in a living organic unity.

The concept of "untranslatability" is useful, not only in offering an
abstract theoretical criterion of poetic value, but in directing attention
to the relationship between concrete elements in particular poems (or, for
that matter, in particular dramas, short stories and novels). Like any
other critical concept — unity in variety, coherence, complexity, multi-
valence, catharsis, hamartia — untranslatability too, although it has been
defined theoretically, can be validated only by experience: it is only in
our reading of literary works in the light of untranslatability that we can
test its usefulness and applicability. In regarding untranslatability as
one of the distinguishing features of the greatest poetry, Coleridge
emphasises the outstanding importance of the poem's linguistic form. In his
words, "Poetry is the best words in the best order."[17]

REFERENCES

1. S. T. Coleridge, *Biographia Literaria*, ed. J. Shawcross (1907; London;
    Oxford Univ. Press, 1967), Vol. I, p. 14. All references are to this
    edition and will be given in the body of the text.
2. I take this term from Beardsley, though I use it in a different sense.
    See Monroe C. Beardsley, *Aesthetics* (New York: Harcourt, Brace & World
    Inc., 1958), p. 144.
3. W. K. Wimsatt, *The Verbal Icon* (Kentucky Univ. Press, 1954; London:
    Methuen & Co. Ltd., 1970), p. 214 and the whole chapter on "Verbal
    Style", pp. 201-217.
4. Coleridge, *Shakespearean Criticism*, ed. T. M. Raysor (1907; London:
    Everyman's Library, 1967), Vol. II, pp. 87-88.
5. Gottlob Frege, "The Thought: A Logical Inquiry", translated by A. M.
    and Marcelle Quinton, in *Philosophical Logic*, ed. P. F. Strawson
    (London: Oxford Univ. Press, 1967), p. 23.
6. W. V. O. Quine, *From a Logical Point of View* (New York: Harper & Row,
    1953; 2nd rev. ed. 1961), p. 28.
7. Beardsley, *Aesthetics*, ch. III, pp. 114-147.
8. Wolfgang Clemen, *A Commentary on Shakespeare's Richard III*, translated
    by Jean Bonheim (Göttingen, 1957; London: Methuen & Co. Ltd., 1968),
    p. 232.
9. William Empson, *Seven Types of Ambiguity* (1930; Penguin Books, 1961),
    p. 26.
10. A. J. Ellis, "Intention and Interpretation in Literature", *BJA*, Vol. 14,
    No. 4 (Autumn 1974), p. 319.
11. Dr. F. Cioffi, "Intention and Interpretation in Criticism", *PAS*, 1963;
    rpt. in Cyril Barrett, *Collected Papers on Aesthetics* (Oxford: Basil
    Blackwell, 1965), p. 173.
12. Ibid.
13. Beardsley, *Aesthetics*, p. 25.
14. Wimsatt and Beardsley, "The Intentional Fallacy", in *The Verbal Icon*,
    p. 10.
15. Beardsley, *Aesthetics*, p. 24.
16. *Shakespearean Criticism*, Vol. I, p. 197.
17. That this definition of poetry applies equally to fiction, especially to
    great works of fiction, is well illustrated by the following conversation

with James Joyce as recorded by Frank Budgen:

> I enquired about *Ulysses*. Was it progressing?
> 'I have been working hard on it all day', said Joyce.
> 'Does that mean that you have written a great deal?' I said.
> 'Two sentences', said Joyce.
> I looked sideways but Joyce was not smiling. I thought of Flaubert.
> 'You have been seeking the *mot juste*?' I said.
> 'No', said Joyce. 'I have the words already. *What I am seeking is the perfect order of words in the sentence. There is an order in every way appropriate. I think I have it*'.
> 'What are the words?' I asked.
> 'I believe I told you', said Joyce, 'that my book is a modern Odyssey. Every episode in it corresponds to an adventure of Ulysses. I am now writing the *Lestrygonians* episode, which corresponds to the adventure of Ulysses with the cannibals. My hero is going to lunch. But there is a seduction motive in the Odyssey, the cannibal king's daughter. Seduction appears in my book as women's silk petticoats hanging in a shop window. The words through which I express the effect of it on my hungry hero are: "Perfume of embraces all him assailed. With hungered flesh obscurely, he mutely craved to adore." You can see for yourself in how many different ways they might be arranged'. Frank Budgen, *James Joyce and the Making of 'Ulysses'* (Bloomington: Indiana Univ. Press, 1960), p. 20 (my italics).

To take another example: in his Afterword to the French translation of Malcolm Lowry's great novel *Under the Volcano*, the French critic Max-Pol Fouchet writes:

> On ne peut avoir vécu dans le texte — et nous y vécûmes, désireux de le transmettre — sans savoir qu'il *n'est à peu près pas une phrase de ce texte qui se puisse délier de son allégeance*. Toute phrase s'unit, dans cette oeuvre, au sol, au fond qui la nourrit, ou elle plonge et s'enracine; ... Si, dans votre lecture, vous enjambez des phrases, soyez assuré de rompre une nécessité. Ce livre se réfère à la musique: une note sautée, vous manquez l'accord, la mélodie est fausse. *Vous n'avez pas le droit de rien omettre*. Le tissage, la trame, la texture sont d'un grain tel qu'à les desserrer vous élimez l'ensemble.
> Malcolm Lowry, *Au-dessous du volcan* (Gallimard, 1959), p. 626 (my italics).

Bibliography

Abrams, M. H. *The Mirror and the Lamp: Romantic Theory and the Critical Tradition*. New York: W. W. Norton, 1958.

Aristotle. *On the Art of Poetry*, in *Classical Literary Criticism*, translated by T. S. Dorsch. Penguin Books, 1965.

Beardsley, Monroe C. *Aesthetics*. New York: Harcourt, Brace & World, 1958.

Bond, Donald F. "The Neo-Classical Psychology of the Imagination", *English Literary History*, Vol. IV (1937), pp. 245-264.

Booth, Wayne C. *The Rhetoric of Fiction*. Chicago & London: Univ. of Chicago Press, 1961, 1970.

Brett, R. L. *Fancy and Imagination*. The Critical Idiom 6. London: Methuen, 1969.

Brown, J. E. (comp.) *The Critical Opinions of Samuel Johnson*. New York: Russell & Russell, 1926, 1961.

Brown, S. G. "Observations on Hume's Theory of Value", *English Studies*, Vol. XX (1938).

Budgen, Frank. *James Joyce and the Making of 'Ulysses'*. Bloomington: Indiana Univ. Press, 1960.

Chambers, E. K. *Samuel Taylor Coleridge. A Biographical Study*. Oxford, 1938.

Chapman, G. W. (ed.). *Literary History in England, 1660-1800*. New York: Alfred A. Knopf, 1966.

Cioffi, D. F. "Intention and Interpretation in Criticism", *PAS*, 1963; rpt. in Cyril Barrett, *Collected Papers on Aesthetics*. Oxford: Basil Blackwell, 1965, pp. 161-183.

Clemen, Wolfgang. *A Commentary on Shakespeare's Richard III*, translated by Jean Bonheim. Gottingen, 1957; London: Methuen, 1968.

Coburn, Kathleen (ed.). *Inquiring Spirit*. London: Routledge & Kegan Paul, 1951, chs. III, IV, V, containing excerpts from Coleridge's published and unpublished writings on language, logic, philosophy and literary criticism.

Cohen, Ralph. "David Hume's Experimental Method and the Theory of Value", *Journal of English Literary History*, Vol. 25 (1958).

Coleridge, S. T. *Biographia Literaria*, ed. J. Shawcross. 2 vols. London: Oxford Univ. Press, 1907, 1967.

Coleridge, S. T. *Notes and Lectures upon Shakespeare and Some of the Old Poets and Dramatists, with Other Literary Remains, Complete Works*, edited by Shedd, 1871.

Coleridge, S. T. *Shakespearean Criticism*, edited by T. M. Raysor. 2 vols.
    London: J. M. Dent, Everyman's Library, 1930, 1967.
Dennis, John. *An Essay on the Genius and Writings of Shakespeare* (1712), in
    Works, edited by Hooker, Vol. II.
Dixon, Peter. *Rhetoric. The Critical Idiom 19*. London: Methuen, 1971.
Eliot, T. S. *Selected Essays*. 3rd ed. London: Faber & Faber, 1951.
Eliot, T. S. *Selected Prose*, edited by John Hayward. Penguin Books, 1953,
    1965.
Eliot, T. S. *On Poetry and Poets*. London: Faber & Faber, 1957.
Eliot, T. S. *The Use of Poetry and the Use of Criticism*. London: Faber &
    Faber, 1933, 1964.
Ellis, A. J. "Intention and Interpretation in Literature", *BJA*, Vol. 14,
    No. 4 (Autumn 1974).
Empson, William. *Seven Types of Ambiguity*. Penguin Books, 1930, 1961.
Frege, Gottlob. "The Thought: A Logical Inquiry", translated by A. M. and
    Marcelle Quinton, in *Philosophical Logic*, edited by P. F. Strawson.
    London: Oxford Univ. Press, 1967.
Haas, W. "The Theory of Interpretation", in *The Theory of Meaning*, edited by
    G. H. R. Parkinson. London: Oxford Univ. Press, 1968, 1970.
Hobbes, Thomas. *A Briefe of the Art of Rhetorique*. London, 1637.
Hobbes, Thomas. *Body, Man, and Citizen*, edited by Richard S. Peters. New
    York, N.Y.: Collier Books, 1962.
Hobbes, Thomas. *The English Works of Thoman Hobbes of Malmesbury*, collected
    and edited by Sir William Molesworth. London: John Bohn, 1840; 2nd rpt.
    Germany: Scientia Verlag Aalen, 1966.
Hobbes, Thomas. *Leviathan*, edited by C. B. Macpherson. Pelican Books, 1968.
Horace. *On the Art of Poetry*, in *Classical Literary Criticism*, translated
    by T. S. Dorsch. Penguin Books, 1965.
Howell, W. S. *Logic and Rhetoric in England, 1500-1700*. New York: Russell
    & Russell, 1961.
Jones, Peter. "Another Look at Hume's Aesthetic and Moral Judgments", *The
    Philosophical Quarterly*, 1970.
Johnson, Samuel. "John Dryden", in *Lives of the English Poets*, introduction
    by Arthur Waugh. 2 vols. London: Oxford Univ. Press, 1973, Vol. 1.
Johnson, Samuel. *Preface to Shakespeare*, in *English Critical Texts*, edited
    by D. J. Enright and E. De Chickera, London: Oxford Univ. Press, 1962.
Johnson, Samuel. *Selected Essays from The Rambler, Adventurer and Idler*,
    edited by W. J. Bate. New Haven and London: Yale Univ. Press, 1968.
Jonson, Ben. *Timber, or Discoveries* (1625-35?), in *Critical Essays of the
    Seventeenth Century*, edited by J. E. Spingarn, 1968. 3 vols. Vols. I,
    pp. 17-64.
Joyce, James. *The Portable James Joyce*, edited by Harry Levin. New York:
    The Viking Press, 1947.
Kallich, Martin. "The Associationist Criticism of Hutcheson and David Hume",
    Studies in Philosophy, Vol. 43 (1946).
Kallich, Martin. *The Association of Ideas and Critical Theory in Eighteenth-
    Century England: A History of a Psychological Method in English
    Criticism*. The Hague, Paris: Mouton, 1970.
Kivy, Peter. "Hume's Standard of Taste: Breaking the Circle", *BJA*, Vol. VII
    (1967).
Lodge, David. *Language of Fiction*. London: Routledge & Kegan Paul, 1966,
    1970.
Merchant, Paul. *The Epic. The Critical Idiom 17*. London: Methuen, 1971.
Mossner, E. C. *The Life of David Hume*. Oxford: Clarendon Press 1954; rpt.
    1970.
Noxon, James. "Hume's Opinion of Critics", *JAAC*, Vol. 20 (1961).
Osborne, Harold. "Hume's Standard and the Diversity of Taste", *BJA*, Vol. 7
    (1967).

Quine, W. V. O. *From a Logical Point of View*. New York: Harper & Row, 1953; 2nd rev. ed. 1961.
Richards, I. A. *Coleridge on Imagination*. London: Kegan Paul, 1934.
Richards, I. A. *The Philosophy of Rhetoric*. New York, London, 1936.
Ryle, Gilbert. "John Locke", in *Collected Papers*, Vol. 1. *Critical Essays*. London: Hutchinson, 1971.
Ryle, Gilbert. *The Concept of Mind*. London: Hutchinson, 1949; rpt. 1960.
Rymer, Thomas. *A Short View of Tragedy* (1692), in *Critical Works*, edited by Zimansky.
Snyder, Alice D. *Coleridge on Logic and Learning*. New Haven: Yale Univ. Press, 1929.
Strauss, Leo. *The Political Philosophy of Hobbes*. Chicago: Chicago Univ. Press, 1952.
Sugg, Redding S. Jr. "Hume's Search for the Key with the Leathern Thong", *JAAC* (1957/58).
Swift, Jonathan. *Gulliver's Travels*. London, 1726. Book 3.
Sidney, Philip. "An Apology for Poetry", in *English Critical Texts*, edited by D. G. Enright and E. De Chickera. London: Oxford Univ. Press, 1962.
Thomas, Keith. "The Social Origins of Hobbes's Political Thought", in *Hobbes Studies*, edited by K. C. Brown. Oxford: Basil Blackwell, 1965.
Thompson, J. A. K. *The Ethics of Aristotle*. Penguin Books, 1953, 1965.
Thorpe, C. D. *The Aesthetic Theory of Thomas Hobbes: With Reference to His Contribution to the Psychological Approach in English Literary Criticism*. New York: Russell & Russell, 1964.
Voltaire. "L'Appel à toutes les nations de l'Europe" (1761), in *Oeuvres Complètes*, edited by Moland, Vol. XXIV.
Voltaire. "Du théâtre anglais", in *Dictionnaire Philosophique*.
Voltaire. "Lettre à l'Académie Française", in *Oeuvres Complètes*, Vol. XXX.
Wilson, Edmund. "Marcel Proust", in *Axel's Castle*. New York: Charles Scribner, 1931.
Wimsatt, W. K. *The Verbal Icon*. Kentucky Univ. Press, 1954; London: Methuen, 1970.
Wimsatt, W. K. "Verbal Style", in *The Verbal Icon*, pp. 201-17.
Wimsatt, W. K. and Beardsley, "The Intentional Fallacy", *ibid.*, pp. 3-18.
Wood, Anthony à. *Athenae Oxonienses*, edited by Philip Bliss. London, 1817, Vol. III.
Woolf, Virginia. *The Common Reader: First Series*. London: The Hogarth Press, 1925; rpt. 1968.

Index of Names